REMOVAL MEN

WRITTEN BY M. J. HARDING
WITH JAY MILLER

T0347907

8 November – 10 December 2016
The Yard Theatre

COCKAYNE

Cast

In alphabetical order

George	Barnaby Power
Beatrice	Clare Perkins
Mo	Mark Field

Credits

Written by	M. J. Harding, with Jay Miller
Directed by	Jay Miller
Designed by	Bethany Wells
Music composed by	M. J. Harding, with Jonah Brody
Lighting and projection by	Joshua Pharo
Sound by	Josh Anio Grigg
Movement direction by	Project O
Casting by	Lotte Hines
Assistant director	Ruby Thompson
Stage manager	Bethan McKnight
Assistant stage manager	Lizzie Laycock
Videography and production photography	Caleb Whissun-Bhide
Publicity photography	Ben Hopper
Publicity design	Kia Tasbihgou and Rida Hamidou
With additional text by	Barnaby Power, Clare Perkins and Mark Field

First produced by The Yard Theatre.

The first run of *Removal Men* was supported by
Arts Council England, Arts Patrons Trust, The London Community
Foundation and Cockayne Grants
for the Arts, and Unity Theatre Trust.

BARNABY POWER
George

Theatre includes: *The Destroyed Room* for Vanishing Point, *Narrative* (Royal Court Theatre), *A Midsummer Night's Dream* (Edinburgh Lyceu), *Casablanca: The Gin Joint* (Gilded Balloon Edinburg, Theatre Dejazet Paris), *Bedroom Farce* (New Wolsey Theatre), *Somersaults* (National Theatre of Scotland), *Interiors* for Vanishing Point (UK & International tour), *The Perfect Child* (Glasgow Oran Mor), *The Girls of Slender Means* for Stellar Quines Theatre Company, *Twelfth Night* and *Comedy of Errors* (Royal Shakespeare Company), *The Wonderful World of Dissocia* (National Theatre of Scotland, Royal Court Theatre), *Laurel and Hardy*, *Faust*, *Trumpets and Raspberries* (Edinburgh Lyceum), *Vanity Play* for Fuel (Battersea Arts Centre), *I Am Dandy* for the David Gale Company, (Edinburgh International Festival), and *Edward Gant's Amazing Feat of Loneliness* (Plymouth Theatre Royal).

Radio includes: *Stamp Collecting With Legs*, *Be Prepared*, *Inside Alan Francis*, and (writer) *Self Storage*, all for BBC Radio 4.

CLARE PERKINS
Beatrice

Clare trained at Rose Bruford College on the community theatre arts course, graduating in 1985. She then worked for several years in Theatre in Education, and is very proud of this work with new writers in great companies; most notably, Theatre Centre, Perspectives, The Women's Theatre Group. Clare has since worked with Almeida Theatre, Tricycle Theatre, Young Vic, the Royal Court, National Theatre, Shared Experience and many more. She played the original Lizzie in *Stamping, Shoutin and Singing Home* by Lisa Evans, and was part of the original company in Double Edge Theatre company's seminal production *Ragamuffin*. Clare will be playing the role of The Ringmistress in Visible's *Roundelay* at Southwark Playhouse in Spring 2017.

Film and TV includes: *Family Affairs*, *All in the Game*, *Clapham Junction*, Bafta-winning *Pig Heart Boy*, *Holby City*, *EastEnders* and *Damned.* Clare has worked with Ken Loach (*Ladybird, Ladybird*) and Mike Leigh (*Secretes and Lies*), and won best Actress for *Bullet Boy* (screen nation, Dinard). Clare has worked extensively in Radio drama, playing Mel in the BBC World Service soap *Westway* for 8 years, and was recently part of the BBC Radio Drama Company.

Clare is a Patron of the youth arts charity Brixton Inclusive.

MARK FIELD
Mo

Theatre includes: *The Rubenstein Kiss* (Nottingham Playhouse), *The History Boys* (National Tour), *The Conquest of the South Pole* (Rose Theatre Kingston, Arcola), *The Grapes of Wrath* (Chichester Festival Theatre & English Touring Theatre), *An Inspector Calls* (National Theatre International Tour), *The Critic* (Chichester Minerva Theatre), *Vincent River* (West End, New York), *Everyman in his Humour – Read not Dead* (Shakespeare's Globe Theatre) *Mad Funny Just* (Theatre 503), *The Revenger's Tragedy* & *Henry V* (Old Red Lion Theatre), *Wedding Day at The Cro-Magnons* (Soho Theatre), *Carries War* (Sadler's Wells Theatre), *The Promise* (Mercury Theatre) *24 Hour Plays* (Old Vic Theatre).

Film/TV/Radio includes: *Fortitude – Season 2* (Sky Atlantic), *Brideshead Revisited* (Miramax), *Lawn of the Dead* (Curve Films), *How Not to Live Your Life* (BBC Television), *Doctors* (BBC Television), *Model Planes* (FFFilms), *Jim* (Mellow 9), *Doctor Who* (BBC Radio).

Directing includes: *August Osage County* (Bancroft Theatre), *Tartuffe* (Yardley Theatre), *Days of Significance* (Crescent Theatre), *Model Planes* (FFFilms), *Are You OK* (London Film Collective) *Cat On A Hot Tin Roof* (RADA).

Mark trained at Oxford School of Drama. He has won the Alan Bates Award, the Old Vic New Voices Award and has been nominated 'Best Actor' at the Off West End Awards. He is also a guest Director at RADA.

M. J. HARDING
Writer

M. J. studied Anthropology at Goldsmiths College, and was classically trained as a musician, before co-founding the band that became Fat White Family.

M. J. began his career as a dramatist in 2009, when he completed the Royal Court Young Writers Programme and began writing for performances in warehouses, squats and galleries across London, including LimaZulu, Topophobia and Anatum's Abode.

Removal Men is M. J. Harding's first full-length work for theatre.

JAY MILLER
Director

Jay Miller is Founder and Artistic Director of The Yard Theatre, which he founded in 2011 in collaboration with Practice Architecture and a team of volunteers. Prior to founding this, Jay had been making work in the North of England with West Yorkshire Playhouse, Arc Theatre and Live Theatre.

Jay's credits for The Yard Theatre are *The Mikvah Project* written by Josh Azouz, which played a sold-out, extended run and received critical acclaim ("Miller's assured direction delivers maximum poignancy" ★★★★ The Stage), and *LINES* written by Pamela Carter ("Directed with finesse by The Yard Theatre's properly talented artistic director Jay Miller" ★★★★ Time Out). *Removal Men* is Jay's third directorial credit for The Yard Theatre.

In 2011, Jay was invited to train as part of the National Theatre's Directing Course, and in 2013 Jay was named by The Guardian as one of the most influential people working in culture today. He also won the British Council Creative Entrepreneur Award 2013, part of the h club 100, for which he travelled to Brazil with the British Council to expand his international network and share ideas.

BETHANY WELLS
Designer

Bethany is a performance designer working across dance, theatre and installation, with particular interest in site-specific and devised performance. With a background in architecture, she enjoys exploring spatial dramaturgy and how space communicates through time in performance.

Recent work includes: *Removal Men* (The Yard Theatre), *Dark Corners* (Battersea Arts Centre), *Seen and Not Heard,* Complicite Creative Learning, (Southbank Centre), and the ongoing *Other Acts of Public WARMTH,* a wood-fired mobile sauna and performance space, commissioned by Compass Live Art and touring throughout 2016/17.

Theatre includes: *Desire Paths* (Third Angel), Sheffield Crucible Fun Palaces, *TANJA* (UK tour), *FADoubleGOT,* (UK tour), *Assisted Suicide: The Musical* (Southbank Centre), *The Factory* (Royal Exchange Young Company), *THE FUTURE* (Company 3, The Yard Theatre), *10,000 Smarties* (Old Fire Station), *FUSE* (Sheffield Crucible Studio), *Late Night Love* (Eggs Collective), *Live Art Dining* (Live Art Bistro), *Race Cards* (Selina Thompson), *Correspondence* (Old Red Lion Theatre), *Dancing Bear* (West Yorkshire Playhouse, Contact Theatre), *A Local Boy* (UK tour), *Partus* (Third Angel).

JONAH BRODY
Composer

Jonah Brody is an International award-winning composer, writer and multi-instrumentalist. He has collaborated with artists and performers in India, Taiwan, Indonesia, Bangladesh, Canada and Japan as well as in London and around the UK. Now based in East London, he performs regularly around the UK and Europe with psychedelic dance bands Loose Meat and Super Best Friends Club, and composes for film and theatre. His writing for folklorist Sam Lee earned him a Mercury Prize nomination and won Songlines Album of the Year 2016. His current work includes making music for award-winning storyteller Ben Haggarty. He has also written music for *Motherland* (Young Vic, House of Lords) and for projects at the V&A Museum and British Museum.

Jonah has previously worked with Music in Detention, making music and performance in Immigration Removal Centres, and he currently collaborates with Rosetta Life, creating music with and for victims of strokes and dementia, in hospitals around London.

He did fieldwork in Bali on Shadow Puppetry and sacred art, and he would like you to buy him an ice cream.

JOSHUA PHARO
Lighting and Projection Designer

Joshua works as a Lighting and Projection Designer across theatre, dance, opera, music, film and art installation.

Recent credits include: *Burning Doors* (Belarus Free Theatre), *Broken Biscuits* (Paines Plough), *THE FUTURE* (Company Three, The Yard Theatre), *Contractions* (Sheffield Crucible); *Julie* (Northern Stage), *We're Stuck!* (China Plate), *Giving* (Hampstead), *Iphigenia Quartet, In The Night Time (Before The Sun Rises), Medea* (Gate Theatre), *The Rolling Stone* (Orange Tree Theatre), *The Glass Menagerie* (Nuffield Theatre, as Video Designer), *The Merchant of Venice, Wuthering Heights, Consensual* (Ambassadors Theatre), *The Crocodile* (Manchester International Festival), *One Arm* (Southwark Playhouse), *The Trial Parallel, A Streetcar Named Desire Parallel* (Young Vic), *Amadis De Gaulle* (Bloomsbury Theatre), *Beckett Season* (Old Red Lion Theatre), *The Deluge* (UK Tour, Lila Dance), *Usagi Yojimbo* (Southwark Playhouse), *Pioneer* (UK Tour, Curious Directive), *I'd Rather Goya Robbed Me of My Sleep, No Place Like Home* (Gate Theatre), *Thumbelina* (UK Tour, Dancing Brick).
www.joshuapharo.com

JOSH ANIO GRIGG
Sound Designer

Josh Anio Grigg is a producer, sound designer and artist from London. Grigg completed a Drama, Theatre and Performance degree at Roehampton University of Surrey in 2008. He has designed sound for many spaces across London as well as creating and performing music in festivals across Europe.

Theatre and performance includes *Love* (National Theatre), *i ride in colour and soft focus, no longer anywhere* (Dance Umbrella), *Beyond Caring* (The Yard Theatre, National Theatre, UK Tour, Chicago), *Made*

Visible (The Yard Theatre), *Parallel Macbeth* (Young Vic), *Lines* (The Yard Theatre), *Fuck the Polar Bears* (Bush Theatre), *Three Studies in Flesh for a Female* (European Tour), *The Mikvah Project* (The Yard Theatre), *Anarchy and Religion* (Jermyn Street Theatre), *Judgement Day* (Emmanuel Centre).

PROJECT O
Movement Directors

Project O (the collaborative supernova between Alexandrina Hemsley and Jamila Johnson-Small) make work that aims to continually address, reevaluate, intervene, comment upon, resist and celebrate the fallout from being born black, mixed and female in 21st Century UK.

In the folding, seemingly endless weight of structural racism (obvious or latent) and white supremacy that has rendered so many invisible and unheard, the politics of Project O are intimate and urgent. They craft choreographic scores and environments to celebrate, challenge and exorcise. Their work is driven by an engagement with dance practices but the creative outcome includes works ranging from shows for theatres to performance lectures, free schools and DJ sets. Project O experiment with alternative ways their bodies can be present and visible (on stage or off), and ways they can be present and visible in our bodies for themselves. One of Project O's compositional enquiries is around inviting audiences to consider their own shifting positions and identities – an attempt to acknowledge that all are complicit in these systems of oppression.

LOTTE HINES
Casting Director

As Casting Director, theatre includes: *Junkyard* (Headlong), *Pride and Prejudice* (Open Air Theatre Regent's Park), *Boys Will Be Boys* (Headlong, Bush Theatre), *The Weir* (The Lyceum Edinburgh), *La Musica* (Young Vic), *Brenda* (The Yard Theatre), *The Glass Menagerie* (Headlong), *Pride and Prejudice* (Sheffield Crucible), *The Boy in the Striped Pyjamas* (Chichester Festival Theatre), *The Absence of War* (Headlong), *The Crucible* (West Yorkshire Playhouse), *Another Place* (Plymouth Theatre Royal), *The Island* (Young Vic), *Pests* (Royal Court Theatre), *Dirty Butterfly* (Young Vic), *The Little Mermaid* (Bristol Old Vic), *We are Proud to Present...* (Bush Theatre), *To Kill a Mockingbird* (Open Air Theatre Regent's Park), *Medea* (Headlong) and *Pieces of Vincent* (Arcola Theatre).

As Casting Associate, theatre includes: *Harry Potter and The Cursed Child* (Palace Theatre), *The Seagull* (Open Air Theatre Regent's Park), *Tipping the Velvet* (Lyric Hammersmith, Royal Lyceum Theatre Edinburgh), *Bull* (Sheffield Crucible). As Casting Assistant, theatre

includes: *Hamlet* (Barbican) and *A View From The Bridge* (Young Vic).
Film includes: *Above* (London Calling), *Kotchebi, Cla'am* and *The Kaiser's Last Kiss.*

RUBY THOMPSON
Assistant Director

Ruby trained at The Royal Central School of Speech and Drama and the University of Manchester, and has worked for Punchdrunk Theatre, Hull Truck Theatre, Theatre Royal Wakefield and the BBC.

Directing credits include *Ten Foot Tales* (Hull Truck Theatre), *Happy Birthday Without You* for Papermash Theatre (Tricycle Theatre/ Paines Plough's Roundabout), *Boxes* (Contact Theatre) and *Green Forms* (The John Thaw Studio). Ruby is one half of Broccolily Theatre, a Hull based company creating new work by local people, for younger audiences.

Ruby is the Resident Assistant Director at The Yard Theatre, and is a part of the Associate Artists team.

BETHAN MCKNIGHT
Stage Manager

Bethan trained in Stage Management at Mountview Academy of Theatre Arts.

Her credits include: *The Deep Blue Sea* (National Theatre), *The Marriage of Figaro and Alcina* (Longborough Festival Opera)*, Firebird* (Trafalgar Studios 2), *Bug* (Found 111), *Talkback 2016* (Kali Theatre), *RooseVElvis* (Royal Court Theatre) and *Roaring Trade* (Park Theatre).

LIZZIE LAYCOCK
Assistant Stage Manager

Lizzie has worked in theatre for over ten years. Having originally trained as an actress, she has always had a passion for live performance. She went on to study stage management and has been working in this area ever since. She has also had the opportunity to work in other areas such as wardrobe and lighting, and has worked on a variety of productions ranging from musicals and children's shows to new works such as Zach Helm's *Good Canary* (Rose Theatre Kingston) directed by John Malkovich.

Built in 2011 by Founder and Artistic Director Jay Miller, The Yard is a multi-award winning theatre and bar based in a converted warehouse in Hackney Wick, overlooking the Queen Elizabeth Olympic Park. The Yard Theatre provides a safe space for artists to grow new ideas, and for audiences to access outstanding new work at affordable prices.

"One of London's most exciting new theatres" **The Guardian**

We actively seek out new theatre makers and new audiences. We nurture new artists and help to discover new talent. We help artists produce new work, by offering a platform that enables theatre makers to take risks.

In our short existence we have had significant success. This includes transfers to the National Theatre for *Beyond Caring* and *Chewing Gum Dreams*, and numerous awards including two Peter Brook Empty Space Awards. Success has also led to partnerships with leading theatres and organisations; recent partners include the Young Vic, Royal Court Theatre, National Theatre and HighTide Festival Theatre.

"The most important theatre in east London" **Time Out**

The Yard Theatre encourages audiences to take risks on new work. We do this by making work about the people in our locale, keeping our ticket prices low and by offering our local community opportunities to be involved in the making process.

Alongside the theatre, we run a programme of events, including music nights which fill our bar and contribute to our unique atmosphere. The Yard Theatre also manages Hub67, a community centre in Hackney Wick - a place for neighbours, young people and creative ideas.

The Yard Theatre brings artists and audiences together in an exciting environment where anything becomes possible.

Recent productions include:

- *Beyond Caring* by Alexander Zeldin, which transferred to the National Theatre and has recently completed a national tour ("quietly devastating" ★★★★ *The Guardian*)
- *The Mikvah Project* written by Josh Azouz, directed by Jay Miller, which played a sold-out, extended run ("Every moment feels rich with meaning" ★★★★ *Time Out*)
- *LINES* written by Pamela Carter, directed by Jay Miller, which received substantial critical acclaim ("directed with finesse by The Yard's properly talented artistic director Jay Miller" ★★★★ *Time Out*)
- *Made Visible* written by Deborah Pearson, which sparked lively debate ("a serious examination of racism and the inadequacies of liberalism" ★★★★ *The Guardian*)

Artistic Director	Jay Miller
Executive Director	Lucy Oliver-Harrison
Finance and Operations Manager	Jack Haynes
Theatre Producer	Ashleigh Wheeler
Marketing Manager	Rida Hamidou
Technical Manager	Rhys Denegri
Music and Events Producer	Dan Hampson
Local Programmer	Katherine Igoe-Ewer
Development Officer	Gareth Cutter
Bar Manager	Luke McCoy
Marketing and Producing Assistant	Lara Tysseling
Technical and Buildings Assistant	Jessica Barter
Front of House Coordinators	Zack McGuiness
	Greg Barnes
Resident Assistant Director	Ruby Thompson
Bar Duty Managers	Katie Andrew
	Stephen Love
	Stephen Love
Artistic Associates	Josh Azouz
	Jude Christian
	Greg Wohead
	Cheryl Gallacher
	Dan Hutton
	Alexandrina Hemsley
Casual staff	Phoebe Hill
	Enrica Miller
	Dimitris Chimonas
	Frankie Regalia
	Isabella Javor
	Maya Carter-Birch
	Scarlet Sherif
	Sari Shrayteh
	Alex Roe
	Dominic Coates
	Otamere Guobadia
Board	Christopher Daniel
	Greg Delaney
	Antony Gummett
	Jay Miller
	Robin Saphra
	Carolyn Ward
Individual Supporters	Francesco Curto
	Greg Delaney
	Nicholas Hytner
	Heather Perkins

Supporters

Why is Removal Men at The Yard Theatre?
By Jay Miller

Removal Men follows a short but determined tradition at The Yard Theatre of making work which allows us to look contemporary western culture straight in the eye. And what *Removal Men* sees there is our inability to love in a world of wire fences. A system of inequality that has left us brutalised and confused. A crisis of compassion.

All this has been intensified by that other crisis, the one whose name has become so familiar as to be horrifyingly mundane: the migration crisis. In *Removal Men*, we set out to make a show which used an IRC and the broader context of the migration crisis to explore the idea of a systemic cultural 'removal'.

This removal runs deep. It affects all of our collective decisions, creating indecision and confusion. And yet it does not seem to form part of a contemporary conversation. There are too few people examining the causes and consequences of a world where it has never been easier to communicate and yet we still cannot connect; a world where we are bombarded with images of suffering, numbing our empathy; a world in which hierarchies seem so entrenched that they render love (in whatever form that may take) almost powerless.

Removal Men may at times be uncompromising, but it is not without hope. It is at The Yard Theatre because it attempts to look at the world we find ourselves in today, a world that is divided and scared, where love is distorted, confused – and confusing. And in this attempt, we hope to create conversation and feelings that may lead to a change.

Is this naïve idealism?

Probably.

But naive idealism is what's needed right now.

The process
By M. J. Harding

On February 29th 2012 I was involved in a direct action in Bedford Hospital, where we prevented the removal of a female who had been on hunger strike at Yarl's Wood IRC. Driving back to London, I realised I recognised the male officer who'd been at her bedside; he seemed like the kind of stoner I'd grown up with in Essex, and before long I was writing scenes in which two male officers discussed self-help while in control of a female in the back of a van.

For a couple of years, the show gave birth to itself in various warehouses and squats around London. Sometimes alone, sometimes with others (Jonah Brody, Nick Owen, Julia Voce, Jonny Liron). I found the form starting to evolve – a dream state, in which a quietly violent institution on the edges of our consciousness could be manifested in front of an audience for a couple of hours. At the time of writing, most of the places I showed the work have shut, as the economics of London currently precludes them. This show would not have been possible if it did not have access to nights where the boundaries between art forms, politics and audience members was so deliberately ignored.

In 2015, Jonah Brody and I presented a scenario with songs to Jay from The Yard Theatre, who asked us to create a version for Jerwood First Drafts (a mini-festival of work in progress sharings) later that year. Following that, *Removal Men* was commissioned. Jay and I agreed on a collaboration to build a plot with three acts, and with Jonah, more songs were added. The process of creation included a dramaturgical week, an actors' workshop, composition and arrangement sessions, many emailed drafts and arguments, and then a rehearsal period, asking the actors to improvise and find the necessary range in the show which you now hold in your hands.

A note on the show
What is Removal Men?
By M. J. Harding

Removal Men wants to create situations in which characters from Birchanger Immigration Removal Centre test our empathy. While writing it, one of the questions I had in mind was something like *"why is it so much easier to go to therapy than change the law?"*, or, perhaps, *"what happens when the workshop leader dies?"*.

This show has a spiritual aspect, part of which comes through the text, and part through the performance style. I wish there was another word for spiritual. I mean a few things, not dogma, not God. I have personal questions about whether anybody is a villain, or heroic; whether human needs are universal, and if they are, what deprives us of them. I ask whether we are really able to re-organise ourselves in relation to social structures. As far as staging this play is concerned, I try to ask these kind of questions beyond the dialogue; in the organisation of actual bodies on a stage – the bodies of Beatrice, George, Mo and Didi. To this end, I've written scenes which make accessible various states of consciousness. Moments of trance, or the Commedia Lazzo, or lamentation. Songs have been included to bring about other states which are harder to name. Some of the show is meant to be played naturalistically, but not much of it. If you're an artist making this play, some of this might influence your rehearsal style.

The injustice of the immigration detention system

Detention became legal via the Immigration Act 1971 as a tool for immigration control, which allowed people to be held in Immigration Removal Centres or prisons for an undetermined amount of time.

According to the UK Border Agency, the written reason for detention should be given to the detainee. The six possible reasons given for detention are:

1. 'You are likely to abscond if given temporary admission or release;

2. There is insufficient reliable information to decide on whether to grant you temporary admission or release;

3. Your removal from the United Kingdom is imminent;

4. You need to be detained whilst alternative arrangements are made for your care

5. Your release is not considered conducive to the public good;

6. I am satisfied that your application may be decided quickly using the fast track asylum procedures.'

UK Border Agency, Enforcement Instructions and Guidance, Chapter 55, section 55.6.3

There has been a rapid growth of the UK's detention estate. In 1993 there were 250 places available in Immigration Removal Centres. In 2016 there are over 3,300 places across 11 Immigration Removal Centres and 2 holding facilities, outsourced by the Home Office to several private companies. As Stephen Shaw in his 2016 report into vulnerable people held in a detention centre acknowledges, *'It is open to question how far a set up of multiple suppliers in competition with one another allows for the development of a more systemic approach or for sharing – and learning from – best practice.'*

The Home Office *Enforcement Instructions and Guidance* states that *'detention must be used sparingly, and for the shortest period necessary'* (Chapter 55:3). However the UK is one of only a few countries in Europe that does not have an upper time limit on legal detention. In Ireland the limit is 21 days, France it's 45 days, in Belgium 2 months and in the USA the limit is 180 days. A 2015 cross-party inquiry into the use of detention in the UK argued that detention is not being used as a last resort: *'we detain far too many people unnecessarily and for far too long. The current system is expensive, ineffective and unjust'.* (2015:4) The report argued a 28 day time-limit should be implemented.

In May, 2016, the Government had an opportunity to pass through this 28 day limit in the Immigration Act 2016. Despite these strong recommendations, the limit was not passed. The recommendation was also that pregnant women should never been detained, and this was not carried through either, though pregnant women should now only be detained for a maximum of 72 hours, or up to a week with ministerial ascent. Between 2011 and 2014 the UK Government paid nearly £15 million in compensation following claims for unlawful detention.

Sources:

Shaw, Stephen (2016) *Review into the welfare in Detention of Vulnerable Persons: A report to the Home Office*

All Party Parliamentary Group on Refugees & the All Party Parliamentary Group on Migration (2015) The Report Into the Inquiry of The Use of Immigration Detention Centres in the UK, The A B Charitable Trust & Oak Foundation

Women for Refugee Women (2014) *Detained: Women asylum seekers locked up in the UK*, Girma, Marchu et al. (ed.)

Immigration Act 2016, Part 3: Enforcement

Thanks

Removal Men owes its existence to the time and support of a huge number of organisations and individuals who have believed in the work to our core – not least Clare, Barney and Mark, our amazing cast of actors, who have approached a show both risky in subject matter and revolutionary in form with a phenomenal open heartedness and an acute critical eye.

Like the text, the music and movement you'll witness tonight have also been built upon a bedrock of fierce collaboration. Mike has worked with longtime musical partner Jonah Brody, a brilliant musician and composer and one half of the original 'Removal Men', to create the music of this show, which is unlike any we've heard in a club or gig before, let alone a theatre. Project O, a dance duo who audiences of The Yard Theatre will know, have made their movement direction debut with this show, creating a movement language built with the performers' bodies.

As ever, we have worked with a team of talented designers and team members who have been fundamental to us working out what the show is, as well as what it might be. Bethany, our designer, has built a world for the characters both comforting and strange. The Joshes Grigg and Pharo, our sound and lighting designers respectively, have once again created whole new theatrical languages for The Yard Theatre using projectors, walkie talkies and smoke. Ruby, our assistant director, has tirelessly researched IRCs, Druze culture, and nonviolent communication to contribute to the world-building that's happened in the room. Bethan, our stage manager, has kept everything in order – a not inconsiderable task. The team at The Yard Theatre have contributed their ideas and their energies for the last 18 months to a project which has at times seemed almost ludicrously ambitious. And finally, and importantly, we have had the invaluable support in our research of people with direct experience of the UK immigration system, both as migrants and as officers.

Removal Men owes its existence to the time and support of a huge number of organisations and individuals, including Women for Refugee Women, Jess at Yarl's Wood Befrienders, Rob – a befriender, Lira Peterson – an ex detainee, Darakhshan Khursheed – an ex detainee, Josephine – an ex detainee (deported in August 2016), Deborah – a current detainee, Emily Ntshangase-Wood, Rosie MacPherson and the rest of the *Tanja* team, Dara, Barbora Benesova, SBC Theatre, Sally Dean, Olivia Charlesworth, Oliver Long, Dan Cottrell, Bethan McEvoy, Sarah Graham, Emily Jeeves, Kathleen Hood, Sarah Readman, Tom Mothersdale, Lorna Gayle, David Beames, Howard Gooding, Erik Perera, Harriet Wistrich.

Our thanks also go to Women for Refugee Women, Jess at Yarl's Wood Befrienders, Rob (a befriender), Lira Peterson (an ex detainee), Darakhshan Khursheed (an ex detainee), Josephine (an ex detainee, deported in August 2016), Deborah (a current detainee), Emily Ntshangase-Wood, Rosie MacPherson and the rest of the Tanja team, Barbora Benesova, SBC Theatre, Sally Dean, Olivia Charlesworth, Oliver Long, Dan Cottrell, Bethan McEvoy, Sarah Graham, Emily Jeeves, Kathleen Hood , Sarah Readman, Tom Mothersdale, Lorna Gayle, David Beames, Howard Gooding, Erik Perera and Harriet Wistrich.

REMOVAL MEN

REMOVAL MEN

Written by M. J. Harding with Jay Miller

OBERON BOOKS
LONDON

WWW.OBERONBOOKS.COM

First published in 2016 by Oberon Books Ltd
521 Caledonian Road, London N7 9RH
Tel: +44 (0) 20 7607 3637 / Fax: +44 (0) 20 7607 3629

A catalogue record for this book is available from the British Library.

PB ISBN: 9781786820686
E ISBN: 9781786820693

Cover design by Ben Hopper, Kia Tasbihgou and Rida Hamidou

Characters

BEATRICE

GEORGE

MO

1.1 INCANTATION.

*The officers repeat the words in **bold** as a mantra.*

BEATRICE speaks the entire text right through, as if she's giving a speech.

Some phrases are sung.

The aim is to use the words to reach a state of trance.

Harlow Odeon.

After the war they done it. Harlow got put right up there. Statues, theatres, civic centre.

Leaders

with vision. Pastoral, I call it. Like shepherds. Cuz you need something to do,

Growing up.

When I grew up I took them right at their word. I used that Odeon. We saved up to go.

Mum

wanted us to have a proper education in school – and we did, we did get taught in school – but I loved the

Harlow Odeon.

I was in pain. Whatever pain I was in, films helped. And that is why I make a point of showing films in my

Removal Centre.

I have a little

Girl.

My little girl watches films and I worry. I *worry* about what my little girl sees. I worry about her

Character.

Consuming all them mermaids in bikinis. George? *(Pause.)* George. *(Pause.)* George!

GEORGE: Beatrice?

BEATRICE: I'm trying to work on this pitch mate.

GEORGE: Why are you going on about films?

BEATRICE: The money for the role plays.

GEORGE: Yes.

BEATRICE: They're like films, aren't they, role plays.

GEORGE: Yes, Beatrice.

BEATRICE: But we're in them, we're taking part in them.

GEORGE: Yes, Beatrice.

BEATRICE: What's Molly watching though? She's watching mermaids.

Why ain't she watching business women in suits?

MO: *(Quietly.)* Fuck suits.

GEORGE: You let her wear make-up and all that. Nice shoes.

BEATRICE: It's not about her appearance.

GEORGE: What's it all about?

BEATRICE: Is what I'm saying going over your head a bit?

GEORGE: Nah I think I understand, I've got a wife and that.

BEATRICE: I want to make sense when I pitch for this money. You, me, Mo, all the other officers, in our hard environment. We've changed, haven't we.

GEORGE: Oh, yes. We've changed alright.

BEATRICE: How do I make our change clear, to the people from the Cornhill Foundation?

(The music darkens.)

MO: Fuck suits.

BEATRICE: What'd you say?

GEORGE: He says he doesn't like suits.

MO: I fucking hate all suits.

BEATRICE: Yes but we have to work with them, don't we.

GEORGE: He's alright.

BEATRICE: Is he? *(Pause.)* Mo? *(Silence.)* Do you two watch music videos? Women, writhing, wriggling? Do you enjoy watching them?

GEORGE: Erm…

BEATRICE: Do you?

GEORGE: Some of them have more artistic merit, don't they.

BEATRICE: Do they? Forget all that. I have to think of something else to tell the money people. I have to tell them facts.

The music surges.

BEATRICE: My daughter comes to see me in my office sometimes.

M & G: Her girl comes in to watch us work.

BEATRICE: And I tell her this is Mummy's centre.

M & G: We protect the females in our care.

BEATRICE: My daughter she sees what leadership means, what it means.

M & G: The staff have just one simple goal.

ALL: Care.

ALL: *(Spoken.)* The Home Office want these women | removed. These women | are at a difficult moment in their lives. We help keep them | safe.

A silence. Then BEATRICE leaves; MO and GEORGE explode into joy.

1.2. CLUB LICK.

Club Lick, a sex club in Walthamstow. It is late at night.

MO enters first. He has a vodka bottle.

GEORGE enters second. He is carrying a big red butt plug.

GEORGE: Well what mate?

MO: What?

GEORGE: What mate?

MO: She's thrown us out.

GEORGE: Throw who?

MO: She shouted.

GEORGE: At me.

MO: No, she shouted, 'you, out.'

GEORGE: Me, she meant. She wants you to stay with her. Go back in.

> *MO raises his hand; when GEORGE goes to hi-five him, MO withdraws the offer.*

GEORGE: Now, I know there's a man through there wearing nothing but his socks.

MO: I stood there next to him.

GEORGE: It's good for you.

MO: I stood next to the man in the socks. 'The Best Dad in the World.' I looked from his socks to her and back again, and I was / overcome with

GEORGE: On a technical point I am your supervisor. In the difficult environment, in which we work, am I not your favourite manager?

MO: I don't do favourites, George, my friend.

GEORGE: Now, moving on from that remark. I'm going to let you in on something. I brought you here partly 'cause I knew it would be good for you. But also, you are a secret weapon. It just so happens that you are a serious penetrative object. And that, at Club Lick, counts for quite a lot. Look at my body.

MO: You've got quite a small cock.

GEORGE: Have I?

MO: It's interesting here. Thanks for inviting me.

GEORGE: Thank you for coming, Mo. It's the second best sex club in the borough of Waltham Forest. *(Pause.)* Are you doing someone at the moment? *(Pause.)* Who are you doing? Two weeks ago, you'd have gone ballistic in there. This whole building would have been raided by the army, trying to get you out. Something's up. *(Pause.)* Alright, I'll leave you alone. Let me talk about myself. Do you know what it was that first brought me down to Thursdays at Club Lick?

MO: Was it that you found your life at home a crushing disappointment?

GEORGE: The workshops. It was the Compassionate Officer Programme. Got me right back in touch with my sexuality. I realised, if I was going to rekindle the flame at home, I needed to find out somewhere safe, what my authentic sexuality was.

GEORGE touches himself. MO looks perturbed.

GEORGE: What? I can touch my own cock.

MO: What's that you've got?

GEORGE holds up his butt plug.

GEORGE: It's part of my awakening. This is a butt plug. I'm past the training ones. I'm considering signing a contract with The Geebie.

MO: What contract?

GEORGE: If I sign it, I have to put this right up there. I'm hesitant. I refuse to make any decisions without due reflection.

MO: George.

GEORGE: Mo.

MO: George, look. I stole her Russian vodka.

GEORGE: *(Snatches it greedily.)* You're on report. *(Drinks.)* Why did you perform this theft, Mo?

MO: This label, it's interesting. When she said 'get out', I had it in my hand. I panicked.

GEORGE: An excellent excuse. You're promoted.

MO: We're a long time dead, aren't we.

GEORGE: Donuts don't deserve what?

MO: What?

GEORGE: What don't donuts deserve?

MO: I don't know what donuts don't deserve

GEORGE: What a donut. Ha ha! *(Drinks.)* Fine surroundings. I like this room. I like the leather sofa on my back. It relaxes me. After the stress and the crying of the centre. If you like, I'll suck your knob.

MO: Will you?

GEORGE: You want me to suck your knob? Actually, I've changed my mind. *(Pause. He grabs MO's testicles.)* Just imagine, what it would be like, if we could participate in the Compassionate Officer Programme, every day. Imagine the empathy.

MO: Are you going to sign the contract?

GEORGE: It costs a lot of money. I'd have to give her my savings.

MO: You're really dedicated to this awakening, aren't you? Has anyone ever done you up… there?

GEORGE: Yeah. Why?

MO: Did you lie on your back or your front?

GEORGE: Oh mate. *(GEORGE stands.)* Who said I was lying down?

MO: And what's that? On the wall? Is it blood?

GEORGE: Could be. Hard to tell in this light. Might be shit. Why don't you get drunk?

MO: Because of what happens when I drink.

GEORGE: Oh yes. What about drugs? Same thing?

MO: Depends on the drug.

GEORGE: Tell me why you're down. I'm actually serious. Go on. Tell me. It might be helpful. I can tell. I can tell that you are down. Do you need to do some Nonviolent Communication?

GEORGE snorts the vodka.

MO: You know when your brain can't stop thinking about a situation?

GEORGE: Didn't know you had someone fresh on the go. Doesn't even tell me when he's doing someone new. Thought he was my mate. How long?

MO: How long what?

GEORGE: How long was it?

MO: How long was what?

GEORGE: Months, weeks, hours, seconds, what?

MO: Weeks, I think.

GEORGE: Weeks can hurt the most. You hurt?

MO: Yes. *(Pause.)* I need to come up with a plan.

GEORGE: What's gonna happen? *(Silence.)* Ey? What's gonna happen? *(Silence.)* I understand. It's happened to me. The conditions of love. We all have to meet them. It feels like… it's like a… uh… uhh… oh. *(Silence.)*

MO: I've realised. I have no sense of place.

GEORGE: Mate. I can offer you a sense of place. *(He shows his arse.)* Walthamstow!

MO: One day, I might go abroad. I'll sit with some people who ask, where are you from? I'll stand up and say, Bishop's Stortford. 'Oh!' they gasp. 'How remarkable! I've heard so much about the wrinkled contraceptives in the river Stort. They're like jellyfish. And' – they lean close – 'is it really true? Was a homosexual man beaten in the loading bay of Wilko's for no reason?' 'Yes,' I'll say, 'it's true. Stortford is like the pyramids, or Machu Pichu. We can purchase crack cocaine from a man called Spanish. Well, we no longer can, because he's in prison for shouting racist abuse in a synagogue.'

GEORGE: Abuse. Oh. I hate abuse. *(Eagerly.)* What did he say?

MO: 'Paki scum' or 'coons', I can't remember. I'd be surprised if it was accurate. He was drunk and full of joy.

GEORGE: I believe that is racist. I believe there are powerful workshops all about that kind of thing.

MO: Do you?

GEORGE: Can I share a text message with you I received, recently, at work?

MO: No.

GEORGE: I need very much to show you this text message I received. It demonstrates the power of the groups. Please look, please. *(Thrusts it.)* Look. 'What do you call a Jamaican in glasses?'

MO: Are you racist?

GEORGE: Me?

MO: You shouldn't be racist.

GEORGE: I'm not racist. Are you?

MO: I'm not.

GEORGE: How do you know?

MO: I have solid evidence.

GEORGE: Show it to me.

MO: I can't.

GEORGE: Please. Read it out. I need to share this moment with you. What do you call a Jamaican in glasses?

MO: No.

GEORGE: What do you call a Jamaican in glasses? Rasta-four-eye!

MO: *(Bellows, Patwa.)* RASTAAAA FOUR EYYYE!! *(Pause.)*

GEORGE: It's not racist. Is it. It's not saying anything negative. He's smart, Willsy. He learned about compassion.

MO: Willsy is racist.

GEORGE: It is a bit racist, isn't it. I need to spend time with you. It's important for the development of your personality.

MO: Can you help me, George?

GEORGE: I can help you. Sit down. I want to help you. I love you, Mo. Come on. That's it. *(Pause.)* Read this one out. How many Mexicans does it take to change a light bulb? Go on, please. Read it.

Mo: I'm worried I'm going to do something terrible at work.

GEORGE: How many Mexicans does it take to change a light bulb?

Mo: I don't know.

GEORGE: Only Juan!

MO: Very good.

GEORGE: What you need to do, with me, is relax. Relax.

MO: You know. One thing. We have got a motte and bailey castle.

GEORGE: A what?

MO: A motte.

           (Together.) Ahhhh!

GEORGE: True.

MO: We have got that. And Hatfield Forest, where once, Henry VIII hunted.

GEORGE: Good dogging up there

MO: Up where?

GEORGE: Great dogging up near where Henry hunted. Where that Korean cargo plane crashed in the middle of the night. If you like I can help you with your suffering.

MO: Help me.

GEORGE: Do you know why the Koreans crash their planes?

MO: What?

GEORGE: 'Why is that, George?' Because Koreans are particularly hierarchical.

MO: Tell me how this is helping. I want to listen.

GEORGE: They love the guv'nor. That's why they crash their planes.

MO: Can you just explain how you are helping?

GEORGE: I read about it in a book about being a famous genius.

MO: Why were you reading that?

GEORGE: I bet you 50p this helps. In Korea, the hierarchy is very strict. Right?

MO: Yes.

GEORGE: So, anyone who tells their guv'nor what to do, is seen as rude.

MO: Yes.

GEORGE: Right?

MO: Right.

GEORGE: If you're a co-pilot, in a cockpit, and you notice that the captain is making some kind of mistake, say,

some arctic ice on the nice Korean wings, and you
fail to tell him, obviously… what's going to happen?
Ey? Ey? With me?

MO: With you where?

GEORGE: Huh?

MO: With you where?

GEORGE: *(Anger.)* That's why Korean planes statistically crash
more often!

MO: I understand.

GEORGE: Thank you. Thanks for understanding me. It's not
racist. It's sociological. Don't ask me what it's got to
do with being a famous genius, I can't remember.
Hierarchy, manners. Manners, silence. Silence, crash.
Now we can go dogging in Hatfield forest. *(Grabs MO,
violently.)* I hate hierarchy. I hate hierarchy. I hate
hierarchy. I fucking hate it. It's deadly. It's a killer. It's
a killer. Don't you agree?

MO: Yes.

GEORGE: Exactly! Hierarchy! You have to watch out for it.

MO: I will. I will watch out for it.

GEORGE: That's why you suffer.

MO: That's why I suffer.

GEORGE: We live in a very violent hierarchy.

MO: Yes. Yes, we do.

GEORGE: Just look at our centre, where we work.

MO: I am. I am looking at it.

GEORGE: Have you ever really sat down and grieved, for a
single day in your life?

MO: I think so.

GEORGE: I bet you ain't. I bet you just skip over it. Stuff it
under the carpet. Because when you were growing
up, someone said, 'real men don't cry. They

think, and they joke, and they work.' It's a fucked up hierarchy, and at the top of it, is a group of traumatised boys. *(Pause.)* They don't like it. *(Pause.)* We have got a choice, haven't we.

MO: Have we? Have I got one now?

Silence.

GEORGE: Always got one. Always got a choice. *(Pause.)* Might not like the choice you have, but you have got one. *(Pause.)* Try and *feel* it mate. *(Pause.)* If you do go through there, can I watch?

MO: I can't. I can't.

GEORGE: Just sit there, and think about what choice you have.

GEORGE goes next door to check with The Geebie. MO slumps down. He's breaking. GEORGE comes back out.

GEORGE: Go on, let her treat you like a feudal peasant in Hatfield Forest. I hate hierarchy Mo, so much. I honestly hate it. It's why they made me supervisor. Because I know about hierarchy. It's the reason I like to be dominated. Because I'm a guv'nor. *(Shouts.)* MO! Take a deep breath, and get in that room. *(Quietly.)* Trust me. This is what you need. While we're here.

MO: Is it what I need?

GEORGE: What's the highest form of human intelligence?

MO: Cars that drive themselves.

GEORGE: The highest form of human intelligence is to observe without evaluation. That's Krishnamurti. Go and see The Geebie.

MO: I don't need to follow orders.

GEORGE: But I'd like to watch, through that gash in the painting there. I'd like to watch your bum being struck by a plastic rod. *(GEORGE suddenly grabs MO, violently.)* Mate. I'm hammered. *(Shouts.)* I'm going to have a hell of a shit tomorrow! Wear the gas mask.

The gas mask with the amyl nitrate. Go on, it'll make you puke.

Yeah. *(Silence.)* Mo. Is it… No.

MO laughs, loudly.

Music starts; it sounds sad, haunting.

GEORGE: It's good! Working with you, mate! It helps me. Helps me… get to grips…

MO leaves, the other way, not going to The Geebie.

GEORGE notices MO is going the wrong way, but says nothing.

To music, MO and GEORGE start to dress as security officers.

1.3 SMALL MAN.

GEORGE: I like to be the small man
Forgive me
I like to go out when I can
Forgive me
I like to buy the same as Clive buys
Forgive me
And when I die, I'd like to have one person cry…
Forgive me, forgive me, forgive me.

MO: I'm here inside this woman's cell
Forgive me
I know her country was like hell
Forgive me
I put my walkie talkie onto quiet
Forgive me
I hope that later when she's free she looks out over cross the sea
She touches her body and thinks about me
Forgive me, forgive me, forgive me, forgive me, forgive me

19

1.4 OUTSIDE DIDI'S DOOR.

At the centre. There has just been an incident. The scene is still. Too quiet. They are outside Didi's door. MO is holding the handle of a mug. The rest is missing. MO is still a little drunk, it shows in his speech. He has a bit of blood on him.

MO: She's cut.

GEORGE: Who?

MO: Didi.

GEORGE: Well, right, let's go in and have a look.

MO: It's alright. We can wait.

GEORGE: No we can't. She's not very big.

MO: It's fine, relax.

GEORGE: We need to go and help her.

MO: Cordelia's coming.

GEORGE: First response?

MO: Don't go in there.

GEORGE: It's an emergency. I'm your supervisor.

        (MO blocks GEORGE.)

MO: Can you wait?

GEORGE: Look me in the eyes. Come here. No. Look me in the
        eyes.

MO: My mug's broken too.

GEORGE: Which mug?

MO: My favourite one with the Frisbee dog on it.

GEORGE: Right. Ready?

MO: Please don't. Listen to me. Wait for Cordelia.

GEORGE: What's wrong with you?

MO: *(MO gestures.)*

GEORGE: You got shock or something?

MO: Shock. *(He smiles.)*

GEORGE: I'm not letting you in there with shock. You won't be able to handle it. *(Pause.)* Why won't you let me in?

MO: Okay. Go in if you want.

GEORGE: Are you pulling my knob? Is she actually injured?

MO: Yes.

GEORGE: What's wrong with you? Oh no.

MO: What?

GEORGE: I can't do any heavy lifting.

MO: Why not?

GEORGE: I'm reluctant to share the reason.

MO: Share your reason.

GEORGE: It's not funny.

MO: I know it's not. It's serious.

GEORGE: I'm pathetic. I hate this job. All month, nothing happens, it's boring. The day I try and make it interesting…

MO: Explain why you can't lift anything up.

GEORGE: Last night, I signed the contract. She can make it buzz off the internet. I can't do any heavy lifting.

MO: Why don't you remove it?

GEORGE: There isn't time now is there.

MO: Yes there is. Cordelia's coming. Go and take it out in the loo.

GEORGE: I'll go in and check on Didi. Put her in the recovery.

MO: It's alright, she used to be in a militia. She's not scared of death.

GEORGE: Enough. Move.

MO: She's ain't scared of death. Where's Cordelia? *(He gets his radio.)* Cordelia? *(Silence.)* Cordelia? *(Silence.)* I need to do the report.

GEORGE: You're right. Beatrice is going to need to know about it. Get the story sorted out right now.

MO: What it was

GEORGE: What?

MO: She didn't want to go on the plane

GEORGE: You came in to check before

MO: I came.

GEORGE: You came in to check before she

MO: I came.

GEORGE: You came in to check before she… *(Pause.)*

MO: What?

GEORGE: Yeah.

MO: Well that's that then.

GEORGE: That is that. That is that. That is that. Move your body.

MO: George.

GEORGE: *(Agitated.)* What?

MO: What you said last night about hierarchy in Korea.

GEORGE: What?

MO: We can be better people.

GEORGE: Why are you saying this to me now?

MO: I made a… decision. I made a decision! Yes…

GEORGE: Oh no. Is this my fault?

MO: Uhh…

GEORGE: What have you done?

MO: What do you mean? I ain't done nothing.

GEORGE: *(Listens.)* Didi? You in there? *(Silence.)* This is a terrible situation. I *have* to go in Mo. I have to go and help her.

MO: I told her that her plane will be after lunch.

GEORGE: You told her that, okay.

MO: It's true, isn't it?

GEORGE: Think so. I haven't looked at today's yet.

MO: You told me you're compassionate last night.

GEORGE: I am! *(Listens.)* She isn't making a noise now.

MO: No.

GEORGE: *(Knocks.)* Didi!

MO: No.

GEORGE: *(GEORGE chucks MO out of the way and goes in. He comes out. He's shocked.)* Oh my God. I can't handle that lot on my own. Where the fuck is Cordelia? Mo, call an ambulance.

MO: I don't know where my phone is.

(GEORGE gives MO his phone. MO is suddenly distressed, paralysed.)

MO: What should I say?

GEORGE: What?

MO: I don't know how to describe it. What should I say?

GEORGE: Yes you do. I'm going to go and use her tights as a tourniquet.

(GEORGE goes back in. MO, drunk, stares at the phone. He doesn't call the ambulance. Dialogue is shouted from inside.)

GEORGE: Didi! *(Pause.)* Didi! Is there anything I can say to bring her back round?

MO: What?

GEORGE: She's barely responding. What's her nickname?

MO: Didi is her nickname, George.

GEORGE: Where's she from?

MO: She's Druze.

GEORGE: What's Druze?

MO: It's what she is! It's her religion!

GEORGE: What's her favourite film?

MO: Titanic.

GEORGE: Right. Didi? Didi? Can you hear me, babe? Do you
            want to watch Titanic?

MO: Her old man's a pigeon racer.

            (GEORGE comes out. He's now covered in blood, too.)

GEORGE: Well that's life Mo. People race all sorts of things. Have
            you called the ambulance?

MO: Yes.

GEORGE: Good. Fuck's sake! Get some mints or something from
            the machine. You smell like a Polish salad.

MO: I have nothing to hide.

GEORGE: I know you haven't. You have nothing to hide. Can
            you pull yourself together a bit?

MO: Don't tell me what to do!

GEORGE: Come on mate. Give me some help. Club Lick. Takes it
            out of me nowadays. *(Pause.)* How are you feeling?

MO: What?

GEORGE: I'm not going back in there on my own. Face that mess.
            Not for this money. You made the bed mate. Go and
            lie in it.

            *(MO suddenly explodes into violence. He grabs GEORGE and
            slams him against the wall by the throat. He is about to tear
            into Didi's room, but can't, so instead tears into whatever he's
            closest to, before coming back and starting to destroy the space.)*

*(The music has already started. **Therapy Storm**; quotes from therapy workshops, soundscapes, and over it, noises of violence.)*

(GEORGE lies on the floor, stunned.)

(MO's movement becomes a dance. He leaves.)

1.5. TRAUMA.

Outside Didi's door, shortly afterwards. Cordelia has been. Didi is in medical.

GEORGE is traumatised. He's lying on the floor. BEATRICE enters.

BEATRICE: What's going on?

GEORGE:　What?

BEATRICE: What?

GEORGE:　How are you?

BEATRICE: Why are you lying on the floor?

GEORGE:　Am I?

BEATRICE: You're lying on the floor. What just happened in Didi's room?

GEORGE:　There was an incident. How's Molly? Did she enjoy her party?

BEATRICE: You were there. You saw what happened.

GEORGE:　Oh yes, that's right. Has she used the clippers I got her?

BEATRICE: No. I found them to be quite an inappropriate present. Can you get up? We're in the corridor. What if someone comes through and sees you lying there? It looks weird.

GEORGE:　You're alright though, are you? Slept alright?

BEATRICE: I'm not going to hit you. Relax. Do you need a hug?

GEORGE:　Do you have a need to give me a hug?

BEATRICE awkwardly crouches down, and holds GEORGE.

BEATRICE: Babe. I'm your manager but I'm gonna hug ya. Come here… come here. I'm your manager but… look… you can cry if you want. Nothing wrong with crying, we've been through that. Cry.

GEORGE cries.

Even Cordelia, she was crying. Yes. That's it. Cry, babe.

It's not your fault. It's not your fault. We're all in this together.

GEORGE: What we gonna do? Mo's gone off his rocker out there.

BEATRICE: I know he has. I don't know what just happened. Tell me what happened.

GEORGE: Didi got cut.

BEATRICE: Did he attack you?

GEORGE: I can handle it. I can handle it.

BEATRICE: Tell me. Did Mo just attack you?

GEORGE: No.

BEATRICE: Are you sure?

GEORGE: He didn't attack me. I think he needs to go and have a rest at home in bed.

BEATRICE: I ain't got the staff to let him go home. Now Didi's cut herself we have to all be here. Something might… happen. She's got a lot of friends in here.

GEORGE: I don't want to divert you.

BEATRICE: You're not diverting me. You're the reason I come here.

GEORGE: I'm diverting you. *(Tries to stand.)* I'm fine.

BEATRICE: Stay there. Stay on the ground for a sec.

GEORGE: I know, but

Enter MO.

MO: LOL. Guess what? In the canteen right now. Cornish pasty. *(Mimes.)* Thrown, and I caught it! Caught the Cornish!

BEATRICE: Who threw a pasty?

MO: Oh one of Didi's friends... was a protest. Caught it. Turned it into a game. *(Pause.)* George is on the floor. Sore legs mate?

How are you, Beatrice? Been alright?

BEATRICE gets her radio. MO approaches GEORGE, who flinches away. MO plays with this control.

BEATRICE: Right, first response to the canteen please. There's been a disturbance; they've thrown food at Mo. Put them in isolation.

(To the officers.) Did Didi attack you, George? I know she's quite handy with her self defence.

MO: Didi didn't attack him. He needs a rest.

BEATRICE: What happened earlier?

GEORGE: Please. I can't revisit this morning now.

MO: He doesn't want to go there, Beatrice. He's / wobbly

BEATRICE: We need to know.

MO: Don't interrupt me.

BEATRICE: What?

MO: You always interrupt me when I'm talking.

BEATRICE: No I don't. George, honey. We have to get together and find out why she done it.

GEORGE: Please. I don't wanna hear no violent language.

MO: What's so violent about a cup of tea?

GEORGE: Uhhh...

BEATRICE: A cup of tea isn't violent, George.

GEORGE: Agh, please...

27

BEATRICE: George, waddya mean violent language? Help us out. I need to get an idea of what's happened.

MO: You mean words like... cut, gash, slice, and that?

GEORGE: Uuugh... no!

MO: I will come up with other ways to describe what happened then. How about 'talk'?

GEORGE: Well that depends on what it is that's being said.

BEATRICE: Listen you two. You're both a bit shaken up. Just take a moment to relax.

MO: What's violent about tea, George?

(GEORGE starts to cry again.)

GEORGE: The colonies...

MO: Have you heard of the Bumper Book of Mysteries?

BEATRICE: No.

MO: I think it's what we're lost in, Beatrice. I'll just whisper it to you. Come here.

BEATRICE: *(Sudden anger.)* No, you come *here*. *(Pause.)* Please.

MO goes over and seductively whispers in her ear. BEATRICE looks annoyed.

GEORGE: Look, speak it out loud, I'll just cover up my ears. *(GEORGE covers his ears. MO approaches, and uncovers them.)*

MO: It's alright. I understand. *(Knocks.)* I did knock. Step into her room. There she is, on the bed.

BEATRICE starts taking notes.

GEORGE: Careful, Mo, careful.

MO: In my hand, I have a... uh... receptacle of... warm... brown... colonial... liquid.

BEATRICE: You mean tea?

MO: Good morning Didi, I says, observing out of the window behind her that it has started to rain.

GEORGE: Oh!

MO: I wanted to inform you that your… removal…

GEORGE: Uh! It's too much. Can I go and sit in the loo for a bit?

BEATRICE: I need you here to corroborate, babe. We need to get this sorted out and then we can carry on with our day.

MO: I said… 'just after lunch, myself, and potentially Sheila, will accompany you to the… van?'

GEORGE: Uhh… uh… van… van. It's actually quite an attractive word.

MO: Yeah I know.

BEATRICE: Lads.

GEORGE: What was Didi wearing?

MO: Pair of jeans. Jumper.

GEORGE: Nice.

BEATRICE: Go on, Mo. Continue filling us in.

MO: She lay there, prone, her phone in her hand, wearing jeans.

GEORGE: I can't handle it Beatrice. It's too much. Did the grip on her phone strike you as quite a strong grip? Was it quite firm?

MO: The plastic almost squeaked.

GEORGE: Oh! Too much. Did you hold yourself upright when you spoke? It could be that Didi found it… stimulating… too dominant maybe?

BEATRICE: I'm concerned about the tone of this enquiry.

MO: I held myself upright. Strong.

BEATRICE: Are you sexualising this encounter?

MO: It's helping George cope. He needs it to sound like pornography, because of the level of violence.

GEORGE: Uhh… no. Please, Mo. I don't want to carry on.

BEATRICE: I'm not going to lie, fellas, I am now disturbed. You two, are you turning Didi into an object? When we need to be at our most compassionate? Are you?

GEORGE: How can you ask that, Beatrice? Look at the officer I've become. Just now, I let my manager hold me on the floor while I cried; what better sign of compassion could there be at a time like this?

BEATRICE: Yeah, but I'm not hearing any empathy for the detainee who just injured herself.

GEORGE: You're right.

BEATRICE: I know I am. We've been through a lot together. Now, I'm going to give you one more chance.

MO: What, now? Don't you have to call the Home Office?

BEATRICE: What did you say?

(There is a buzzing sound, as the butt-plug in GEORGE's arse goes off. GEORGE cries in alarm and tries to cope.)

BEATRICE: George? What's happening? Is it trauma? What's that buzzing noise? *(Pause.)* Can you hear it, Mo?

MO: Oh, I know what it is. It's his / remote

GEORGE: It's a private condition, Beatrice... it's not / related

MO: He's been visiting a specialist in Walthamstow / and

GEORGE: Don't tell her! I need the lavatory / please...

BEATRICE: No, stay there, on the floor. I'll get Cordelia to come and help.

GEORGE: No Cordelia!

(A silence.)

BEATRICE: I will be candid with my feelings. I feel... suspicious... I feel suspicious and a little bit upset. I'm trying to establish what just happened to Didi. I don't want to be excluded like this.

GEORGE: It's stopped. *(Pause.)* Right. What were you saying about the Home Office?

BEATRICE: Why can't I find out what's been going on in my own centre?! *(She grabs MO.)* Give me a straight answer. What, you've got something wrong with your arse hole? I don't mind arse holes. I work with enough of them.

MO: George?

GEORGE: Please, Mo, think of the boundaries.

MO: Every Thursday, George goes to Club Lick in Walthamstow, where a woman called The Geebie strikes his buttocks with her yellow plastic rod while she shouts out verses of the New Testament.

BEATRICE: Ha ha!

GEORGE: Uh... Mo, mate...

BEATRICE: I'm a progressive leader. I'm open minded. I thought it was something serious.

GEORGE: It was the truth. I suppose we're honest men. Thanks Mo.

MO: He's got a big red plug stuck up his bum. It's this big. She's making it vibrate remotely.

BEATRICE: That's a bit different. That's bordering on a breach of your contract isn't it? What if you need to do some heavy lifting?

MO: And?

GEORGE: And I gave her your number, so she might call you later.

BEATRICE: You gave her my phone number?

GEORGE: I think I've given her all my savings.

BEATRICE: My phone number.

MO: It's his thing. The Geebie might call you and try and get him the sack.

BEATRICE: If you didn't have such a gregarious track record, you would have the sack.

31

GEORGE: Yes, Beatrice.

BEATRICE: Is this arousing you?

GEORGE: There is a smidgeon of arousal, yes.

MO: He makes that face when he's aroused, it's true.

BEATRICE: How do you know that?

MO: He showed me last night, when he came back into the room.

BEATRICE: *(Pause.)* My work phone number?

GEORGE: Your personal number. It was part of the contract.

BEATRICE: That is the most trivial gesture in the history of violence I ever heard about in my *life*.

GEORGE: Yes, Beatrice.

BEATRICE: *(Shouts.)* WE HAVE TO USHER SOME COMPASSION IN.

MO: I agree.

GEORGE: Me too.

BEATRICE: Go and take that thing out, George. Go and set up the disco. I need to carry on with my day.

GEORGE: Yes, Beatrice. *(GEORGE doesn't leave.)*

MO: You need to call the Home Office about Didi.

BEATRICE: Bless you, Mo. I've got to think about it.

MO: Wait a minute.

BEATRICE: What's up, mate.

MO: You're going to tell them, aren't you?

BEATRICE: Excuse me, if you don't mind. What I decide to do next is my business.

MO: You've got to tell them. We have a duty of care.

BEATRICE: I know we have. What's wrong with you? You still upset babe?

MO: Do you need to do a management training programme?

BEATRICE: Can you advise, why, as a detention custody officer,
           when your the centre manager tries to take control,
           you insist on over-riding her?

MO: You love systems. You fantasise all night about
           systems. You hate people.

BEATRICE: What on earth is happening to you?

MO: You love the pilots of Korea.

BEATRICE: You're on a warning. You've just been given a
           warning.

MO: Sack me then.

           BEATRICE squares up against MO.

BEATRICE: Tell me what to do. One more time. Tell me what to
           do in my centre. You little maggot.

MO: Sack me. I don't care. I don't believe in hierarchy any
           more.

1.6 UTOPIA

BEATRICE: One night I watched TV and it really had me.
           Salvation Army built a camp out in Hadleigh.
           1863, a new camp for sick Cockneys
           But when I told my fella about it he mocked me.
           Watching that show, cut out all the noise,
           Salvation Army cockneys and their factory for toys.
           How innocent they looked, loading toys onto barges,
           How different from my work with the Home Office
           surcharges.
           Gave me an idea, to start a new scheme,
           to usher some compassion in, you know what I mean?

GEORGE: First workshop she got in was the worst.
           Was it the first?

Them teenage acting students, that burst
Into a rage, into the room
Unrehearsed.
They screamed, they threw their knickers
                    Disperse!
Please, disperse.
Jack, the oldest officer, cracked.
He couldn't stand the swearing, and he whacked
– he really whacked –
A teeny in the knackers
and got the sack.

And that's when our guv'nor, Beatrice, went on the attack.

BEATRICE: My mate Elisa smelt the stress in my sweat glands.
She took us in her Audi to see the new wetlands.
She said 'you have to help your staff, cuz they have to serve.'
We talked about it at the marshland reserve.

'The attitude at work I know has been an obstruction,
Yet here we stand, at a marsh for birds, built with old clay from construction.
You can't demand of staff that they have constant contentment,
You can build them a wetland with excavated resentment.'

Gave me an idea, to update my new scheme,
to usher more compassion in, to get the staff clean.

GEORGE: Workshop two, we're all sat in them chairs
– them hairy chairs –
Bloke called Jay 'invites' us, to get all into pairs.
From that point on we all begin to care,
About our role, our rota,
our despair.

I remember, the first time,
we watched a colleague cry.

34

Clive cried in front of all us.

And in his tear, I could see the sky.

BEATRICE: O great, all my officers are crying in silence.

Deep in the bowels of Essex, they think about their violence.

At first I weren't sure what on earth to suggest,

Then I sat down with them, got some things off my chest.

The more we wept, the more we heard our heart beats resound,

How miraculous: the sound of heart beats gets around.

Journalist tried get in from the Harlow Telegraph.

I knew at that point – I'd changed the life of my staff.

I'm glad that my idea, to start a new scheme,

ushered some compassion in, or so it seemed.

GEORGE: Workshop three, a guy called Mike proceeds

To draw up on a whiteboard

the universal human needs

Having seen all of Mike's diagrams, I was set

To say 'I feel hurt, my need for love ain't being met.'

For all these sudden officers, our feelings weren't a threat.

We all relax, re-connect,

I even give up cigarettes.

Then the money ran out.

And Mike left, I regret.

And now I look it all up, by myself, on my own, on the internet.

And then the money ran out,

And Mike left, I regret,

And now I look it all up, on the internet.

BEATRICE takes out her phone.

BEATRICE: *(Spoken)* Hello. It's Beatrice Mustill, from the Birchanger Centre. I need to report, a detainee, Didi

35

Halibi, has injured herself four hours prior to her removal. Yes, that's fine. I'll hold.

The song continues.

BEATRICE & GEORGE:

Now I know these things cost money.
Now I know these things they cost.

BEATRICE: This is how you build a new world

Now I know these things cost money.
Now I know these things they
Now I know these things cost money

BEATRICE: This is how you build a new world.
If they let you bloody build it.

(Spoken, into phone.) Hello?

1.7 THE SOUND SYSTEM.

In silence, MO and GEORGE set up the machine. They are wary of each other.

GEORGE: Shall I smoke you with the machine?

MO: Smoke me.

GEORGE: Stay there, stay there.

GEORGE smokes MO with the machine.

GEORGE: Willsy's ill. *(Pause.)* He's not actually ill. He's skiving. But he knew how to set this lot up with his eyes fallen out from drugs.

MO: Where does this lead go?

GEORGE: Hold it up so I can see. It goes in the speaker.

MO: I know. There are two holes.

GEORGE: Put it in the hole it goes in.

MO puts it in the wrong hole. It makes a horrible noise.

GEORGE: Not that one!

MO: Calm down, please.

GEORGE: I'm not gonna lie to you, my friend. I am
           exceptionally nervous.
           I sing with nerves! My juice sloshes yellow with
           adrenaline! O bum, behave!

MO: Why are you nervous?

GEORGE: Got a few things on my mind.

MO: The money. Is it what your family are going to say
           when you explained where all your savings went?

GEORGE: Yes. Partly, it's my family. Another thing though.
           Earlier, you put your hand around my throat and
           smashed me against the wall.

MO: Oh.

GEORGE: Smashed, that's my personal evaluation. I want to
           put it more objectively. You used force to press me
           against the wall. It hurt. I don't want you to do it
           again.

MO: I won't do it again. I promise.

GEORGE: What will you do?

MO: I don't know.

GEORGE: And then just now you goaded the manager into
           striking your face. Again, shit, goad. How can I put
           that more objectively? You said you don't believe in
           hierarchy.

MO: I'm still here though aren't I.

GEORGE: If we had the staff you wouldn't be.

MO: Come here towards my body.

           (They embrace. It's awkward. Something's changed.)

GEORGE: Mm…

MO: Yeah. *(Silence.)* What's happened?

GEORGE: You've changed. I don't know if you're here or there.

MO: I don't feel well. I don't know what to do. I'm at the edge of the cliff. I told you something might happen.

GEORGE: Tell me what it is.

MO: No.

GEORGE: *(Grabs MO.)* Tell me what it is before it gets any worse.

MO: There's nothing to say.

GEORGE: You're burning through the handkerchief of our night.

MO: What hanky?

GEORGE: Don't you like poetry?

MO: What?

GEORGE: Poetry.

MO: What's that?

GEORGE: *(Angrily.)* I can't remember.

MO: I'm in love with Didi.

          A silence.

GEORGE: No you're not.

MO: I don't want her removed.

GEORGE: I know what she's like. I know how she looks at you when she smiles. It's a fantasy mate.

MO: Is there anything you can think of that might help?

GEORGE: It's all in your imagination. I know, I've been there myself.

MO: It started after the workshops.

GEORGE: Did it? How?

MO: Something happened to my brain.

GEORGE: Did you do it in the normal place? Up the gym?

MO: Don't talk about it like that.

GEORGE: Alright. What is it, about her character, that has you so infatuated? You said something about her gun earlier. Caught your libido, has it?

MO: She showed me a picture. She was in a militia.

GEORGE: What's a militia again? Is it one of them Italian pubs where they bring you all them little plates of food?

MO: That's tapas.

GEORGE: Oh, so it is.

MO: Don't, George. Be serious. When she was younger she was in a militia. She told me her war stories. I can't get her out of my head.

GEORGE: Please, I don't mean to be rude, what is a militia?

MO: You know what a militia is! It's an armed group that fights against a big army.

GEORGE: Oh, one of them. Yeah, I was in one of them once.

MO: When?

GEORGE: What?

MO: When was you in a militia?

GEORGE: What are you on about? I hate Italian restaurants. Give me indigestion. *(Does out of time clapping.)*

MO: Why do you hate me?

GEORGE: Now. These kinds of infatuations, and I do know quite a lot about them, you have to ask yourself: 'How do I know this is real?' There's a little checklist I've made up. Number one, are we actually having it off? Number two, are we talking openly about what's in our heads? Number three, can we make each other laugh?

MO: And what if I tick off your checklist?

GEORGE laughs, for a long time.

MO: What?

GEORGE: I struggle to believe that Didi Halibi would tick my checklist off with you. *(Pause.)* What militia?

MO: The V.R.U.

GEORGE: The V.R.U.? Fuck me. Is it truly fifty fifty? Or is it more like… eighty twenty? Oh God. Not a hundred zero. That's not right mate. Hundred zero is the sacred ratio of abuse and desperation.

Shown you her banner, has she?

MO: Is there anything you can think of that will stop her going on the plane?

GEORGE: Oh, mate. *(Pause.)* It was the workshops, was it?

MO grabs GEORGE again.

MO: George, it's not a fantasy. We're having a relationship. She's the one, mate. We love each other.

BEATRICE enters.

BEATRICE: Aww, that sounds nice. You've set it all up beautifully. Thank you. Shall we have a little dance?

GEORGE: Oh, that's a great idea, let's do a bagatelle. Shall I put the music on?

BEATRICE: Nah, just grunt along to your legs mate. Come on, Mo!

BEATRICE grabs them both. They do a little dance.

BEATRICE: Thank you, fellas. Oh yeah. George, can you get Didi into the isolation for me please, babe?

GEORGE: Oh, it's going ahead is it?

BEATRICE: Yeah, sadly. Home Office haven't given her an appeal. She's got to go with the glucose. It's sad.

GEORGE and MO just stand there. Silence.

BEATRICE: Is there anything I need to know?

GEORGE: Uh. There might be. Help me understand what area you're asking about.

BEATRICE: Disco's all set up I mean? You done it properly, haven't you?

GEORGE: Oh, yeah. I have a question actually. Can we play some different music this week?

BEATRICE: What's wrong with the normal music?

GEORGE: Well, a lot of the women in here are traumatised. And I have a couple of pieces of music which will channel their suffering into the medium of movement.

BEATRICE: You want to be a workshop leader, don't you.

GEORGE: I want to do what's best for the centre.

BEATRICE: I don't know mate. I think we'll need someone with more formal training to handle that kind of event.

GEORGE: I've got the music here. I know I can lead it.

BEATRICE: No, George. Sorry. Mo. How are you?

MO leaves.

BEATRICE: Mate, what's wrong with all the officers today? Are you going through a second puberty?

GEORGE: I don't know what's wrong with him.

BEATRICE: He needs a good sleep.

GEORGE: I can't wait to lie down on my bedroom floor and clench my thighs with the lights out.

BEATRICE: That sounds relaxing.

GEORGE: What are you up to tonight?

BEATRICE: All Bar One. I'm going to get wasted with my retinue, tell them about your shortcomings as a person.

GEORGE: Oh, thanks Beatrice.

BEATRICE: You're welcome. *(Pause.)* What's up with you, George?

GEORGE: Me?

BEATRICE: You've been acting so strangely. Why are you so close to Mo, at the moment?

GEORGE: He's complicated, isn't he.

BEATRICE: You told me once you thought he was an arse hole.

GEORGE: Well, on the surface, he can be like that.

BEATRICE: I've put him on a warning. I've not actually written it, yet. But he's on one. Anyway, I'm thinking I might cancel this disco. All this... disruption. I might just put a film on for them instead.

GEORGE: Potemkin?

BEATRICE: Not Potemkin. Something emotional.

GEORGE: What?

BEATRICE: You know. Maybe the Lion... what's it called? Where he has to take over the kingdom. The Lion... the Lion Prince?

GEORGE: The Lion in the buggy?

BEATRICE: No, it's something else.

GEORGE: I've never heard of it. *(Pause.)* You know, we could do a workshop instead of the disco. I could try and lead it.

BEATRICE: No. We've been through this.

GEORGE: I'm ready. I've been practising at home. I think what's needed in this situation is more participation.

BEATRICE: Do you remember, when the Programme was running, and Colin ended up chucking a chair at Mona? Are you telling me you'd be capable of handling that?

GEORGE: I think I could. Yes.

BEATRICE: No! It would be like a bow and arrow in the hands of a child!

GEORGE: Thank you.

BEATRICE: I'm responsible for a few hundred people, George.

GEORGE: Oh, yes, that reminds me. Didi's flight. Two hours is it?

BEATRICE: Go and put her in separation. There's a chance her friends won't like it. Chucking pasties at Mo. I don't want no one getting dragged.

GEORGE: Yep. That's the process, isn't it.

BEATRICE: Didi's the best dancer we've had here in months. It'll be a shame to lose her at the discos.

GEORGE: I'll tell her you said that.

BEATRICE: Thanks George. You're an ethical worker. You're a good man. You're an apple pie.

2.1 BEATRICE DOES HER NAILS.

BEATRICE is in her office at last, doing her nails, having a rest.

In front of her is her land line.

M – mobile

L – landline

I – ignored

BEATRICE: OMG! I forgot! The goddam application!

She gets out her application.

BEATRICE: This is a bloody good application. If they don't give me the money, the Cornhill Foundation are only suitable for blowing leaves off my fanny with a little leaf blower. *(Pause.)* Is it, 'the Compassionate Officer Programme saw a 65% reduction in violent incidents,' or is it, 'there was, after the initiation of the Compassionate Officer / Programme...' *[L/L.]* Oh you shitting fucking cunt! *[L/L.]* Lyn! How's Croydon? Still got all that traffic? *(Pause.)* Truth is, I don't even know how the detainees got your number. *(Pause.)* No, it wasn't a cake, it was a Cornish Pasty. *[M/I.]* They're upset, aren't they. *(Pause.)* Didi spent eight years in a Lebanese prison, obviously she knows how to make friends. *[M/I.]* Mo. *(Pause.)*

Morris Panrucker. He was just in the canteen. Lyn, my mobile's ringing like billy-o. I just want to see who it is, it's a private number. *[M/G.] (Pause.)* Ugh! No! *(Hangs up.) [L/L.]* Lyn? Oh, please don't speak to Julius. He'll only fine me. Please, not Julius, not Julius... *[Text/I.]* Fine. Go and speak to Julius. *(Holds.)* Julius is a bell-end. *[M/C.]* Cordelia, why aren't you using the radio? Is it that busy in medical again? Oh. *(BEATRICE slumps on the table.)* I literally have Lyn from the Home Office on the other line. *[L/L.]* Lyn? *(Pause.)* Lyn? *[M/C.]* Who's the father? *(Pause.)* Why NOT?! *(Pause.)* Fine. *[T/I.]* Cordelia, tell no one. Who you gonna tell? No one. No one. NO ONE. *[R/G.]* George, please come and see me in my office. Bring tea. *(Reads Texts. Looks annoyed.) [L/L.]* Lyn? *(Pause.)* Lyn? 65% reduction up your cheeks, Lyn! Right up between your pale wet cheeks!

BEATRICE has a moment on her own. She does another nail.

[M/G.] Geebie, I answer to Lyn from the Home Office and in response to your text messages I have never seen a man fart on a cake and I do know what you stuck up George's bottom last night now give him back his savings or your sex dungeon will be taken over by the most aggressive, badly funded outsourcing company since the Mercenaries of Mursili sacked Babylon, FUCK YOUUUUU!!! *[L/L.]* Lyn? *(Pause.)* I was just practising a role play. It's just creativity, isn't it. We can't all be terrified of life, can we?

GEORGE enters.

GEORGE: Beatrice?

BEATRICE: Not now, George.

GEORGE leaves.

[L/L.] I'm going to consolidate my findings and give you my report. You have to trust me. Goodbye.

BEATRICE slumps on the table.

Didi. I apologise. *(She cries.)* I'm going to do what I can for you. I'll do what I can. *(Pause.)* George!

GEORGE enters.

BEATRICE: George. The Geebie said that if I offer you what you want, you'll do whatever I tell you. Is that true?

GEORGE: Yes, Beatrice.

BEATRICE: And what is it that you want?

GEORGE: I don't know.

2.2 PARTY BUNTING

BEATRICE: Do you know what? I'm considering whether to sign off, at the bank, a lovely pink cottage up Manuden. 1731. A cottage. Classic north Essex.

GEORGE: Oh, congratulations!

BEATRICE: Don't congratulate me. Tell me who done it.

GEORGE: Who done what?

BEATRICE: What look am I making on my face?

GEORGE: Don't ask me.

BEATRICE: Are you telling me what I can and can't do?

GEORGE: It's a saying which means 'I don't know'.

BEATRICE: But you do know though.

GEORGE: No I don't.

BEATRICE: Sorry, just a moment. Has anyone seen my bum?

GEORGE: I beg your pardon?

BEATRICE: My bum. Where is it?

GEORGE: It's behind you.

BEATRICE: Where?

GEORGE: Behind you!

BEATRICE: Is this a pantomime?

GEORGE: No, Beatrice.

BEATRICE: Am I a numpty?

GEORGE holds out his hand.

BEATRICE: Why are you holding out your hand?

GEORGE: Because I found your bum. Give me a pound.

BEATRICE takes GEORGE's hand, and kisses it.

BEATRICE: She knows it won't help her case.

GEORGE: Who?

BEATRICE: She's just told Cordelia. I know the Home Office, she said. She knows they won't consider it a factor in her removal. She won't say who did it, because she wants to protect the father.

GEORGE: I think I might be able to guess what you're talking about.

BEATRICE: I've got a womb.

GEORGE: Yes.

BEATRICE: It's not going to be easy for her.

GEORGE: Didi.

BEATRICE: So you did know about it.

GEORGE: Nope.

BEATRICE: Are you trying to protect your friends?

GEORGE: Honestly. I don't know a thing about Didi's pregnancy. *(Pause.)* Can I ask. Are you feeling upset, because your need for... erm...

BEATRICE: Go on. What needs of mine aren't being met?

GEORGE: Your need for...

BEATRICE: How about you? Are you upset?

GEORGE: Upset? How could you ask me that? Think about the special egg.

BEATRICE: Which egg? I hate all this secrecy in our centre. Stop talking in metaphors.

GEORGE: It's a murky little pond.

BEATRICE: Stop it!

GEORGE: Sorry.

BEATRICE: We have to look after Didi, don't we.

GEORGE: Yes we do.

BEATRICE: That's our job. Isn't it. To look after Didi.

GEORGE: Yes, it is our job.

BEATRICE: Seagull?

GEORGE: Could be, yes, could have been a seagull.

BEATRICE: No, it has to be on seagull wing, that's the wing you supervise.

GEORGE: You've narrowed it down, have you?

BEATRICE: Narrowed it down? Seagull wing's your wing! A couple of hours ago you were lying on the floor outside her door! Were you worshipping her?

GEORGE: I was lying there, yes. We all like Didi very much.

BEATRICE: It was you, wasn't it.

GEORGE: Me? Fuck off, Beatrice!

BEATRICE: Who, then? Willsy? Mo? Hamed?

GEORGE: I'm ignorant, Beatrice.

BEATRICE: No you're not. It's why I made you duty manager. Because you're good at gossip.

GEORGE: I don't know who done it.

BEATRICE: Can I let you in on something?

GEORGE: Please do.

BEATRICE: Alright, I will.

GEORGE: Thank you.

BEATRICE: You're welcome.

GEORGE: No, you're welcome.

BEATRICE: Am I?

GEORGE: Yes.

BEATRICE: When I get that money from the Cornfield. I've been considering putting you into training as a workshop leader.

GEORGE: Nah. Don't believe you.

BEATRICE: I want you to lead the Compassionate Office Programme. I want it to be you, mate. I want to train you up. Keep it in the family.

GEORGE: Beatrice, do you know how much that would mean to me?

BEATRICE: Yes, I think I do. All of your empathy. Remember how open everyone was with you? Racist text messages. Bullying. You could just manage it.

GEORGE: I do remember yeah.

BEATRICE: You remember.

GEORGE: It was the happiest time of my life, reading out Willsy's racist text messages. The more racist, the better.

BEATRICE: Think about those texts.

GEORGE: Watching him learn. The most racist... *(Pause.)* We could help a lot of people here.

BEATRICE: I know you have your suspicions. I can see them on your face.

GEORGE: Alright. Alright. I have a suspicion.

BEATRICE: So. Can you do something for me, now? Use all that empathy you've got. Whatever techniques you want. Go and open up the person who you think did this.

GEORGE: What, now?

BEATRICE: Yes. Now. Whatever exercises you want, go and do them. Call it healing. Call it whatever you like. Just go and find the father of Didi's child, and hit them with some compassion.

GEORGE: And then what?

BEATRICE: We can all wipe up the mess together, without anyone having to raise their voice or lie.

GEORGE: I don't know if I'm ready to lead that level of healing.

BEATRICE: Mate, I've been in management most of my life. I know when someone is ready to follow their calling. Where will I find you?

GEORGE: Meet me in the disco room. Meet me in the disco room, at two.

BEATRICE: Thank you. I trust you, George.

GEORGE: Meet me in the disco room, at two. We can get this sorted out. With integrity.

BEATRICE: George, am I being excluded from this centre?

GEORGE: You are a bit, yeah.

BEATRICE leaves.

GEORGE, nervous, gets out his phone.

Marshal Rosenberg video. He leaves, watching it.

–

2.3 PSALM.

*(Very quietly, MO sings **Psalm.**)*

MO: You, by the window, I like how your hair looks.

I would like to comb your hair.

Combing your hair I will be reported.

But I imagine I'm combing your hair.

You, in the kitchen, I like how your food smells.
I would like to eat your food.
Eating your food I will be reported.
But I imagine I'm eating your food.

When you sing with your friends I like how your
song sounds.
I would like to learn your song.
Learning your song I won't be reported.
I become love by learning your song.

You, at the disco, I love how your neck moves.
I would love to kiss your neck.
Kissing your neck I will be reported.
But I imagine I'm kissing your neck.

You, at the basin, I love how your skin glows.
I would love to do your skin.
Doing your skin I will be reported.
But I imagine I'm doing your skin.

When you sing with your friends I like how your
song sounds.
I would like to learn your song.
Learning your song I won't be reported.
I become love by learning your song.

2.4 SOCK.

In the disco room.

MO has found Didi's tights and is sitting with them.

GEORGE enters.

GEORGE: The other day, I went round to see Beatrice and Des, they had a little garden party.

MO: Why weren't I invited?

GEORGE: What it is, although she likes you, you can be quite awkward at parties. It's your sense of humour mate.

MO: My sense of humour is brilliant.

GEORGE: Yes. Anyway, she had some lovely mayonnaise.

MO: I really want to see Didi.

GEORGE: What, in that state?

MO: What's wrong with my state?

GEORGE: Your state is about to violate her.

MO: This is confidence.

GEORGE: You stink. Your breath stinks. Spiritually, you have the appearance of a dictator making a run for the helicopter. Your gaze is an atrocity. What's that you've got there in your hand?

MO: It's a present. I'm going to give them to her.

GEORGE: I'd offer to help you, but I'm worried you'll kick my head in. *(Pause.)* I'm sad about the violence, mate.

MO: I'm sad too.

GEORGE: And Beatrice is sad about the violence as well.

MO: It's been a violent morning hasn't it so far today.

GEORGE: You can say that again.

MO: It's been a violent morning hasn't it so far today.

GEORGE: You can say that again.

MO: It's been a violent morning hasn't it so far today.

GEORGE: Can I help you out with your predicament?

MO: Have you told Beatrice about Didi and I?

GEORGE: No. I'm a man of integrity.

MO: Is that good for you?

GEORGE: It depends.

MO: On what?

GEORGE: I'm sorry? *(Pause.)* Mo, that present. It's… uh… it's very significant.

MO: Is Didi in separation?

GEORGE: Yep.

MO: She won't be leaving today.

GEORGE: Do you know something I don't?

MO: Maybe.

GEORGE: What are you going to do? *(Silence.)* Let me help you.

MO: How can you help?

GEORGE: Your relationship to hierarchy. You're in agony.

MO: I feel fantastic, though.

GEORGE: You're in agony.

MO: I'm not.

GEORGE: You are the embodiment of violence.

MO: I am love.

GEORGE: You feel like love, but you're the embodiment of violence.

MO: I've never been this conscious in my life.

GEORGE: Give me twenty minutes.

MO: I ain't got twenty minutes.

GEORGE: You have got twenty minutes.

MO: Horror won't ensue.

GEORGE: Her leg. All that blood this morning.

MO: I am full of grace.

GEORGE: You know what percentage of our communication is done just through the look in our eyes, don't you?

MO looks out at the audience.

MO: Thirteen percent.

GEORGE: Much, much more than that.

MO: How do my eyes look?

GEORGE: Like they're hiding a rat in their potty.

BEATRICE enters, unseen by MO.

MO: Really?

GEORGE: Yes. I can hardly bear the smell.

MO: How do I know I can trust you?

GEORGE: You say you don't believe in hierarchy no more, but your eyes give you away. Be honest.

MO reflects.

MO: Can you clean them up?

GEORGE: You want me to get rid of the shame in your eyes?

MO: I do feel a little bit ashamed.

GEORGE: Whatever you've got planned, with that much shame in your eyes, it's not going to go very well, is it.

MO: I'm scared.

GEORGE: Let me help. Anything that's worth doing, is worth doing poorly.

GEORGE takes off his shoe, then takes off his sock.

MO: Don't wipe my eyes with your sock, please.

GEORGE: I'm not going to wipe your eyes.

He turns his sock into a sock puppet.

SOCKMO: "Hello, I would like you to call me by my first name, which is SockMorris."

GEORGE: Hello SockMorris.

SOCKMO: "I think you're going to manipulate me, aren't you?"

GEORGE: Well I am manipulating you. SockMorris! Empathy is a very healing phenomenon. Because I know you don't believe me, I'm going to hypnotise you. Turn you into the most loving version of Mo that could ever be imagined. More loving than a... uh... octopus having a shag with a... welly... at the bottom of the Red Sea....

Quickly, GEORGE hypnotises his sock.

Here he is. He's hypnotised. *(Pause.)* He might be quiet for a moment. *(Pause.)* He's in a state of sock.

Silence.

SOCKMO: "Hello Mo. Now I'm hypnotised, I'm going to teach you what love is. Tell me what you mean by love?"

MO: By the picture of the London Eye, first thing Didi ever said to me was, "You are frosted glass". First thing she ever said to me. "You are frosted glass, and I don't know what's behind you." What does that mean?

GEORGE: Can we ground this in reality, please?

SOCKMO: "What is it really in my power to do, today?"

GEORGE: Oh, isn't that a good question, SockMo?

MO: I've tried to help her. It didn't work. I'd like to try again.

GEORGE: You have a difficult relationship with your position as an officer, don't you?

MO: I want to stop her going on the plane.

GEORGE: Why don't you become Didi?

MO: Hey?

GEORGE: Be Didi.

MO: When?

GEORGE: What's she said to you so far today?

MO: Smash your tea. Take off your uniform.

GEORGE: Be her. Become her.

MO becomes DIDI. The music starts. Smoke begins to fill the room.

(M) DIDI: "Smash your tea on the ground. Get your uniform off. My officer, my officer."

Unseen by MO, BEATRICE steps closer, into the role play space.

GEORGE signals to her, she asks for the role play to keep going.

SOCKMO: "Why do you want me to take off my clothes?"

(M) DIDI: "Your uniform's a coward's skin."

SOCKMO: "You want me nude, do you?"

(M) DIDI: "When your skin is off, you help."

GEORGE: What do you want him to do?

(M) DIDI: "Interfere with my removal. I can't go on the plane."

GEORGE: Is that because you love him?

MO suddenly sees BEATRICE.

A moment, while the three acknowledge each other.

They agree to continue playing.

GEORGE: Didi? *(Pause.)* Where have you gone? *(Pause.)*

MO: Didi? I don't care no more.

//(B) DIDI: "I want to know the truth of how you feel."

MO: I can help you with my tea cup, Didi.

(B) DIDI: "What can your tea cup do?"

MO: Stop you from leaving. Stop you from leaving me.

(B)DIDI: "I can't be in England. I must go to Lebanon."

MO: You just put those words in her mouth, she'd say

(B) DIDI: "Your government don't like me. I must go to Lebanon."

SOCKMO: "I realise now that I belong to an immigration removal centre and that there are many people who are influenced /"

MO: I know what she'd say. She'd say, "I know how it works, I was in a militia."

BEATRICE: She'd say "Hand me my ticket, get me on the plane, my family await."

MO: Those are words in her

SOCKMO: "I realise now that I belong to an immigration removal centre and that there are many people who are influenced /"

MO: "Where do I sit, Mo? *(Pause.)* Where do I sit? Where do you want them to find me?"

GEORGE: Say that you cannot help her.

(M) DIDI: "Mo and I found real love. His tea cup is the answer to my life."

GEORGE: Say that you can't help her. That is love.

(M) DIDI: "Mo you know what to do. I don't need to tell you." // *(Repeat.)*

(M) DIDI makes a cutting gesture.

GEORGE: Say that you can't help her because that, that is love.

MO leads on the following lines. GEORGE and BEATRICE join in.

What can I do?

"I am not just a story " she said, by the bed, "I am more than your story."

We do what we want, we can do what we want.

I stayed up all night, and rather than sleep, all the moments in my life I'd made the wrong decision ran before my eyes.

Are you ready for you new life?

*While MO repeats the above lines, GEORGE and BEATRICE
repeat the following, including the (mate.) Eventually, MO
hears what they are saying, and joins in the repetition, without
the (mate.)*

Didi's pregnant (mate), Didi's pregnant (mate), Didi's
pregnant (mate), Didi's pregnant (mate), Didi's
pregnant (mate.)

3.1. DRUZE POP SONG

*A fast, flashy dance number. Combines techno with Druze rhythms. MO, in
a state of wild excitement, sings.*

MO: The first thing to do is to buy a new rug
And fill up the fridge with juices in jugs
I'll cuddle Didi, we'll sing and I'll say,
That mummy and daddy are happy today!

When Didi gets out we can go to the Half Moon
Through to the back room where he plays the folk
tunes
Sit holding hands, at a table, a candle
Holding her belly my foot on her sandal.

How many hairdressers are there in Harlow?
I'll get my hair done like in Monte Carlo
I will look rich at the garden centre
Didi gives birth and I eat the placenta

BEATRICE: Real life don't make that much sense mate
Real life do not make no sense
Real life don't make no

MO: Go down the library and read the kid books
All stories with shepherds and foxes and cooks
pictures of lions and hunters and geese
my child will listen, our love will increase

When it is time to apply for a school

We'll go for that one with the new swimming pool
The school that plays rugby up high on their hill
I'll find a way to afford all their bills.

Move to a flat with a cleaning lady
and bathes every day and who cares for the baby
I'll save all our money, the house will be clean,
We'll eat bags of chicken, I'll buy loads of beans.

We can get married, I'll be a good dad,
The child will grow up without going mad,
If it's a daughter, if it's a son,
It's clear to me that love has won.

– Dance –

GEORGE: I am ready to lead

BEATRICE: Real life don't make no sense

3.2. REMOVAL MEN.

MO: I'm going to be a daddy!

BEATRICE: Thank you Mo. Now, can you remember what we just done in that role play?

MO: Yes. She's going to be released. They release pregnant women.

BEATRICE: What do you have to go and tell her?

MO: That it's not my job to release her.

BEATRICE: That's right.

MO: She's pregnant! I'm a daddy!

GEORGE: We are still security officers.

BEATRICE: What's the last thing she needs?

MO: Any stress.

GEORGE: Any stress at all.

MO: She can't have any stress. *(Pause.)* Oh, mate. She can't have any more stress today.

BEATRICE: Imagine all of that extra pressure. Stress gives us ulcers.

MO: Beatrice. I understand. I understand. I really want to see her.

BEATRICE: I know you do. You need to be a nice strong man. Just finish off the disco set up, with George. Then you can go and see her.

GEORGE: Mate, you're doing really well.

BEATRICE: Let me make a phone call.

MO: Am I? Am I doing well?

BEATRICE: What it is, Mo. We're in an immigration removal centre. There are certain jobs that need doing. This ain't a beach resort. For example, put up that fucking picture of Zidane!

BEATRICE leaves.

GEORGE: Mate, I'll keep you company. I know it's tense.

In another room, we see BEATRICE make several phone calls.

GEORGE and MO pretend to finalise the arrangements for the disco. They're just skiving off, fannying around. GEORGE climbs up on top of the ladder, very high up. He's preparing to do a stunt.

GEORGE: This is nothing. It's nothing.

MO: Go on then, do it.

GEORGE: Once, when I was about thirteen, I rolled my bicycle into the house.

MO: Oh yeah?

GEORGE: Yeah. I cycled round the sofa, past all the crayons on the mat, little Hanny's crayons, over toward the radiator, then, in front of the telly, guess what I done?

MO: What?

GEORGE: A wheelie. All while my dad was making a sanger in the kitchen.

MO: Beetroot sanger?

GEORGE: No. You're out of your head mate. He did like listening to the opera though.

MO: What's that?

GEORGE: Oh, just people singing.

MO: I'll keep my eye out for it.

BEATRICE calls GEORGE, from a different room.

MO fools around, trying to distract GEORGE.

BEATRICE: George, listen. It's not me.

GEORGE: Hello? Hello?

BEATRICE: Hello?

GEORGE: Hello?

BEATRICE: It's someone else.

GEORGE: Oh, hello Brian. I'm at work mate.

BEATRICE: You need to remove Didi.

GEORGE: What's that?

BEATRICE: George?

GEORGE: Hello?

BEATRICE: I need you to remove Didi.

GEORGE: Now, Brian, how many times have I tried to reassure you? There's nothing wrong with being gay.

BEATRICE: I know there isn't.

GEORGE: Good, because there isn't.

BEATRICE: I know there's nothing wrong with being gay.

GEORGE: Well, you should know that, because there isn't.

BEATRICE: I know there isn't. Why do you want to reassure me?

GEORGE: Because there's nothing wrong with it. Nothing at all.

BEATRICE: Did you hear what I said?

GEORGE: Any time you want to have a go on it, you know, bum sex and that. Just let me know. We can get a film out and you can do my bum.

BEATRICE: What sort of film?

GEORGE: Tarkovsky. Something Russian. I like having my mind opened.

BEATRICE: We'll go Cambridge.

GEORGE: I love Cambridge, I love the botanical gardens.

BEATRICE: You're listening?

GEORGE: What's that? You want to know if I'm glistening, Brian? Let me just check.

BEATRICE: You're going to do the removal.

GEORGE: Oh, am I? Let me just check my planner. Thursday?

BEATRICE: Fuck your fucking planner! It needs to be done with compassion. I don't want her getting manhandled if she's pregnant. I'm going to come back and keep Mo distracted.

GEORGE: I suddenly feel a little bit overwhelmed, Brian. Can I have a think about the various options you've given me?

BEATRICE: Think about what might happen if he leaves that room. Think about what happens if Mo leaves that room. Are you thinking about that?

GEORGE: Yes, Brian. I'll think about it.

BEATRICE hangs up.

MO: Who was that?

GEORGE: Don't mind him. *(Exhausted.)* I done a big poo earlier.

MO: Well done. How did you sit?

GEORGE: Head in my hands.

MO: Oh that's just excellent. Reflective.

GEORGE: Oh yeah. Rubbed my face a bit, held my head in my hands, and out it came.

MO: What, in one go?

GEORGE: Yeah, more or less.

MO: Fantastic.

BEATRICE enters.

GEORGE: Beatrice – how are you?

BEATRICE: Me?

GEORGE: Yeah, how are you? Are you well down there? Look, I'm very big.

BEATRICE: Get off that ladder please.

GEORGE: Have you managed to have your lunch?

MO: What did you have? Was it nice?

BEATRICE: There's a protest. I just had to push through a group of them in the corridor. Mo, stay in here with me. They wanna dash your guts at a tree.

MO: I'm going to see Didi.

BEATRICE: You can't go and see her.

MO: No, I'm going now. I'm going out there.

BEATRICE: You can't leave this room.

MO: I don't care.

BEATRICE: You do.

MO: I can't.

MO goes running out to leave.

BEATRICE: Good news, Mo! Home Office have agreed to give her an appeal.

GEORGE: Bingo balls!

Everyone is shocked. BEATRICE and GEORGE because of the lie.

MO: I need to go. I need to go, now.

BEATRICE: Please, stay mate. You can't have a reunion in the middle of a riot.

MO: Didi's safe is she?

BEATRICE: She's in Cormorant. She's fine. It's all the other women who are now at risk. Ban congregations. They'll try and gather round the corridor. What's needed's a formation. Lead it up George.

GEORGE: My days of hitting people are over.

BEATRICE stares at GEORGE. He's not doing what they agreed on the phone.

BEATRICE: Have you got any idea how expensive it'll be if we tell them there's a riot? They'll fine us like we forgot to return a book to their library. Bruv.

MO: I like books.

BEATRICE: Yeah they're good aren't they.

MO: Not all of them.

BEATRICE: True.

MO: I can try and head up the force. I feel empathetic.

BEATRICE: You can't do it Mo. George.

GEORGE: I've turned a corner. I don't want to use violence. I'm a workshop leader now.

BEATRICE: George, if you don't head up the force, Colin will, and Colin doesn't know how to use compassion like you do. If Colin does it, in half an hour there'll be thirty broken bones and the fire brigade charging in past the water cooler, maybe even a riot cops with

GEORGE: I'm not in the right emotional state.

BEATRICE: Fair enough. Best to ask. You've done so well with all of us today. *(Gets her radio.)* Colin to Beatrice.

GEORGE: Alright, fucking hell.

BEATRICE: Relax, don't use bad language, everyone will think your soul's gone mouldy.

GEORGE: I'll go and do it.

BEATRICE: Hairy chest.

GEORGE: I'll go and calm everyone down. I'll use all the compassion I can muster.

BEATRICE: *(To radio.)* False alarm. Hold. *(To GEORGE.)* Thanks.

               (GEORGE leaves.)

BEATRICE: Do you know what I love about having a sandwich?

MO: Please tell me.

BEATRICE: They're quick *(Clicks her fingers.)*

               BEATRICE and MO are left alone together for the first time.

MO: Ha ha! I'm in such a good mood. My God. You know – when you feel this good – and you think – now I've cracked it – now I'm living – I've found out how to live – finally – all that time bored, hiding from everyone – it's gone! I was scared, and now I live! *(Pause.)* Hello!

BEATRICE: Hello, Mo.

MO: Can he do it? I wonder. I wonder what's gonna happen. What do you think is gonna happen?

BEATRICE: It's a shame, in a way, when a protest gets put down. I don't exactly see the use of this particular protest though. What's it going to achieve? Abort your baby?

MO: That's disgusting.

BEATRICE: It's the adrenaline, turns me into a journalist.

MO: For what newspaper?

BEATRICE: Don't worry about it. He'll do it. He'll calm them down. Something in him's changed. He's stronger.

MO: Can I ask you a question?

BEATRICE: Yes you can.

MO: When you did you first decide you wanted to run an immigration removal centre for women?

BEATRICE: When I was thirteen, and I first heard about the risks posed by immigrants to local communities. *(Pause.)* Joking mate. They weren't around when I was thirteen.

MO: What did you want to be?

BEATRICE: I wanted a bank. I wanted to manage a bank or a pub. I wanted a girl, and we'd all live above a bank, or run a pub. The pub would have been called The Goat on the Nut.

MO: Were you quite isolated as a child were you?

BEATRICE: No, not really. Were you?

MO: A bit.

BEATRICE: My family run a fabric recycling business. *(Pause.)* Are you worried about your baby? Having a brown baby?

MO: No.

BEATRICE: Are you sure?

MO: I think it'll be good.

BEATRICE: Molly came home from school the other day with a really beautiful song from Lithuania. Do you want to hear it?

MO: What's it like?

BEATRICE: Come here. See if I can remember it.

BEATRICE brings MO in against her chest. She takes a breath.

MO: Wait. What was that about?

BEATRICE: What?

MO: That. The song. The hug. Are you trying to manipulate me?

BEATRICE: No.

MO: Where's George? What's going on out there?

BEATRICE: Ow. Stop squeezing my bones please Mo.

MO: I don't like it when people try and make me feel differently. It's dishonest.

The music stops. Silence.

BEATRICE: Now I feel blue.

MO: Beatrice? Are you alright? I'm sorry I hurt your hand. I'm learning. I'm going to learn. I have to learn to control my anger. Humans are difficult. I'm going to be a terrible father. Am I in trouble?

BEATRICE: Are you in trouble?

MO: My dad used to hit me when I was in trouble. Then he'd be silent for a while. When I tried to tease him to get him to talk he'd hit me again.

BEATRICE is stalling for time. Using empathy.

BEATRICE: Oh, boy. Your dad used to hit you. You tried to tease him. That sounds painful.

MO: That's right.

BEATRICE: Your dad used to hit you. You feared him.

MO: Where's George?

He approaches BEATRICE again.

BEATRICE: Please don't.

MO hesitates. He's thinking about hitting BEATRICE.

GEORGE enters. He's holding a kitchen knife.

GEORGE: What's happening between the two of you here? It looks like you're about to hit Beatrice in the head.

BEATRICE: I think he is.

MO: It was just agitation.

GEORGE: Was that right? You were about to violate the head of
            our guv'nor?

BEATRICE: Is it safe to go out?

MO: Can you tell us about Didi? Is it safe to go back out
            there?

GEORGE: What kind of state are you in? You cross?

BEATRICE: You came back at just the right time. Is it all calmed
            down?

GEORGE: What were you hoping? You'd bash the guv'nor in
            the head and then what? You'll lose everything!

BEATRICE: What's happened to the ladies?

GEORGE: What's your state, Mo?

MO: What's *happening?*

GEORGE: Won't end well, if you hit her in the head, will it?

MO: I know. I know. I'm tense. I'm very tense.

BEATRICE: Can you just tell us what's happening out there please?

GEORGE: Shouldn't I tell you one to one, Beatrice?

BEATRICE: No. Tell us out loud. Let it out, if it's worth letting out.

GEORGE: I just want to take a moment to chill out. *(Pause.)*
            What I just did was quite demanding. *(Pause.)* It's
            fine. Everything is going back to normal now.

            MO goes to leave.

GEORGE: Mo, wait with us for a moment. It's still a little bit…
            it's a bit early to go out there.

            *BEATRICE makes a signal to GEORGE, to ask what's going
            on.*

            GEORGE replies, 'keep stalling.'

BEATRICE: Isn't it a shame, all that effort we put into the disco,
            having to just cancel it at the last minute?

GEORGE: I know. Let me tell you what happened. They'd taken
            the knives from the Global flavours kitchen.

MO: I want to go and see Didi now. Then I'm going to go home.

GEORGE: They're shouting at me. 'Scum!' 'fascist!' 'Carnivore!'

Do you know what? As I approached them, I'm asking,

'are you feeling angry because you need to protect your friend?'

MO goes to leave.

Just a tick Mo. It's still calming down out there. Just let everyone calm down. Just a minute or two. Yeah?

MO: Uhh… okay. Ha ha. It's like a birthday.

He waits by the door.

GEORGE: It's fine. Just a minute or two. Okay. Thank you. Come sit down.

So, I'm there, in the corridor outside the canteen.

MO is very restless. He is desperate to go out and see Didi.

BEATRICE: Come sit down, Mo.

GEORGE: Mo, what kind of state are you in now mate? How are you feeling?

MO: Jubilant. She's safe. You calmed them down. You're a legend.

GEORGE: Great. I did keep her safe. I appreciate that mate.

BEATRICE: I appreciate your service George.

MO: Yes! Yes you did. Please tell me though. She's all alright, yeah?

In his jubilation, MO is becoming violent again.

BEATRICE: Mo can you calm down a bit babe?

GEORGE: I need you to just take some deep breaths mate. Take some deep breaths. Can you do that?

MO: Yeah. Yeah I can.

GEORGE: There's all these knives pointing at me. I had the kindest eyes. 'Can you tell me, are you upset because your need for protection hasn't been met by one of our officers?'

The way I said it, they just lowered their knives.

'I really want to make sure nobody else gets injured, so we can deal with this properly. Can you tell me what's been bothering you?'

They started to tell Me, and all of that riot energy was dissipated.

BEATRICE and GEORGE look at each other. GEORGE nods.

BEATRICE: Can I go now?

GEORGE: I really need to let you know, mate. I feel very unhappy.

MO: What?

GEORGE: I'm telling you this as your friend.

MO: I know. You look after me. You're a good pal.

GEORGE: The Home Office aren't known for their flexibility, are they.

MO: I know. It hurts. I'm glad she's got friends who'll take a stand for her.

GEORGE: If I hadn't chosen to intervene, Colin would have done a room extraction. You would have gone tearing out there.

MO: You're talking weird mate. Stop it. I mean, can you talk normally?

GEORGE: Talk normally?

MO: Please. Talk like a normal person.

GEORGE: Yes I can.

MO: What was that about a room extraction?

GEORGE: I just gave her to the van people. She's gone, mate. She's gone in the van. She's already at the airport.

MO goes to run out. GEORGE holds him back.

GEORGE: Stay, Mo. Stay. Stay. Breathe. You can't do nothing. We've done the safest, cleanest thing.

BEATRICE: You ain't got a car. You gonna run to the airport?

GEORGE: We've got you mate. We've got you.

BEATRICE: Stay here with us. We're looking after you.

MO runs out.

A silence.

BEATRICE sings 'Keep My Skin.'

BEATRICE: First you find me in the car park,
Take me to the field.
Kiss my hair,
Kiss my stare.

Open up my stomach lining,
In the moon, my guts are shining,
Dash the lot against a tree,
Kill the old me totally.

G & B: But keep my skin.

The music continues while they talk.

GEORGE: I feel horrible.

BEATRICE: I'll speak to you about it later. Go and find Mo, would you?

GEORGE: I've made a decision, Beatrice.

BEATRICE: You've turned a corner?

GEORGE: Yes.

BEATRICE: Let's chat about it after can we?

GEORGE: I resign.

BEATRICE: No!

GEORGE: I do. I resign. I can't do this any more.

BEATRICE: It's alright. We'll start the workshops. I'll let you be the workshop leader.

GEORGE: I can't.

BEATRICE: Tell me about it over dinner.

GEORGE: I made up my mind. I don't make enough money here for the pain it causes.

BEATRICE: Oh dear.

GEORGE: I can come back, I can come back and run the programme. *(Pause.)* Some consultants make five hundred a day. Though it's not about the money.

BEATRICE: What, you're going to set up a freelance consultant post next week? When do you resign?

GEORGE: I don't know.

BEATRICE: I still have to do my pitch. We can train you up here, can't we. And then you can resign.

GEORGE: I'll have a think about it.

BEATRICE: Good lad. Go and find Mo.

GEORGE: Yes, Beatrice.

GEORGE leaves.

MO enters. In his hand he's got some scissors.

He approaches BEATRICE.

Music returns.

BEATRICE: Use the hole inside my torso,
As the chamber for the fire.
Throw in the reports I done,
My audits, wedding ring and tongue.

Light it with your favourite lighter.
Dedication burns flame brighter.
Burn the past, burn the longing.
Burn the memory of the longing.

BEATRICE & MO: But keep my skin.

MO lowers his weapon.

BEATRICE & MO: When the starling sings the morning
Nothing's left except for flesh
Hanging off the fence
The failure of my self defence.

Wrap my skin around your shoulders
Let my fascia touch your dreams
Wander back toward the building
Don't tell no one what it means

To keep my skin.

They dance.

MO: Is your office messy?

BEATRICE: What?

MO: Before I go, can I tidy up your office for you?

BEATRICE: It's alright. We've got a cleaner.

MO: Life's very different now, isn't it. *(Pause.)* When do you need to go and ask for the money?

BEATRICE: What?

MO: When have you got to go and give your pitch to that foundation?

BEATRICE: Tomorrow. I'm going down London.

MO: Do you mind if I help you with it? Before I go home?

BEATRICE: Nah, it's alright. I've got it in the bag, I think.

MO: Really? Are you sure it's as strong as can be?

BEATRICE: Yeah, I'll get some cash for it.

MO: I hope you do. I hope you can carry on all the empathy work, Beatrice.

BEATRICE: I tell you what. Before you go. Why don't you

End.